THE ROMANCE OF THE MENDELSSOHNS

BY THE SAME AUTHOR

Switzerland before Europe. Figuières, Paris, 1919. (Out of print.)

Green-White-Red and Service Stripes. Thesis on the re-establishment of the former arms of the country of Neuchâtel. Cooperative Press, La Chaux-de-Fonds, 1932.

Native Land of Neuchâtel. 1st Volume (30 chronicles, 173 illustrations). Central Printing House, S. A., Neuchâtel, 1934. (Out of print.)

Native Land of Neuchâtel. 2nd Volume (36 chronicles, 120 illustrations) La Baconnière Editions, Neuchâtel, 1935.

AWAITING PUBLICATION:

Native Land of Neuchâtel. 3rd Volume.

Native Land of French Switzerland. 1st Volume.

Illustrated History of the Militia Companies of French Switzerland.

Ladies and Young Ladies. Novels.

Cécile Mendelssohn Bartholdy
née Jeanrenaud, 1817-1853

Painting by Edouard Magnus, the property of the Mendelssohn Bartholdy family.

JACQUES PETITPIERRE

THE ROMANCE OF THE MENDELSSOHNS

ROY PUBLISHERS   NEW YORK

LE MARIAGE DE MENDELSSOHN 1837–1937
(Librairie Payot & Cie, 1937)

TRANSLATED FROM THE FRENCH BY G. MICHOLET-COTE

MANUFACTURED IN SWITZERLAND

Sir,

You ask me for a preface to the book in which you have told the story of Mendelssohn's marriage. But why write a preface for a book which stands so well on its own merits? You bring to it many documents handed down to you from your own family. No more is needed, and — better than any word of mine — the enchanting portrait you have given us of Mendelssohn's wife will inspire all who see it with the desire to read your book.

Believe me, etc.

André MAUROIS.

CONTENTS

LIST OF ILLUSTRATIONS

TO THE READER

Many books have been written about Felix Mendelssohn Bartholdy, whose talent is assured of immortality throughout the world. Biographers or music critics have followed his career from the time of his first works to the hour of his death—some with enthusiasm, some with reserve; but the majority of them, immersed in a flood of learned criticism, have scarcely consecrated a few lines to his delightful and lovely wife, Cécile Jeanrenaud.

It is strange that no one should have thought, until now, of introducing Mendelssohn's wife to his admirers, who have always felt so much sympathy and understanding for the composer in other matters. It is certain that his choice of a partner, described by Sebastian Hensel as being like fresh air and the water of a clear stream, exerted a strong influence on his happy and harmonious destiny. The music critic, Emile Vuillermoz wrote recently: 'When the time came for Mendelssohn to settle down, he set out, like a biblical character, to find a companion worthy of himself.' Surely we should know a little of this companion, the constant comrade of the man who was once Goethe's little protégé, the precocious genius who translated Dante and Terence into rhythmical prose for the old man.

Let us then depart from the tradition of high-sounding eulogies of blue-stockings and female pedants. Wherein lies the true worth and dignity of a woman? For my part, since women find fame so rarely on account of their feminine virtues, I should like to exalt one particularly for her modesty. Allow me, therefore, to speak of a real personality, a being conspicuous only for her distinction, her serenity, her charm and her silence. Let me add to the chorus of praises and the endless accounts of the amazing story of Mendelssohn's life, the one note which is missing.

Into what milieu did Felix Mendelssohn Bartholdy, hailed by Richard Wagner as the purest genius in Germany, marry? In what circumstances did the marriage take place? Mendelssohn himself was a Protestant, and the son of a Protestant, but that did not prevent this same Wagner from turning against him, *after his death*, and attacking him in a most unseemly way in a tendentious pamphlet entitled *Judaism in Music*.

Let us see also what were the origins, the connections and the ancestors of Cécile Jeanrenaud; and what kind of woman she herself was. Let us recall the distinguished figure of her father, a Calvinist preacher whose unpublished letters touch upon so many significant events, great and small; and let us gaze at the lively features of her mother, the pious descendant of a line of Huguenots. And lastly let us see what were the joys and sorrows of that ideal couple, Felix and Cécile, for to celebrate a centenary it is fitting that every fragment of the past should be brought to light and unknown documents made known. As a beginning to our story, we will visit the home country of Cécile Jeanrenaud.

There are in existence about a score of portraits of the composer, of which few have been published. Those reproduced here are either some which have not previously appeared elsewhere, or else are among the most interesting. Those of his wife are, for the most part, quite unknown to the public, and, in common with nearly all her portraits, that by Magnus has never been published.

I would like to thank Mme Frédéric de Steiger-Wach (the grand-daughter of Felix Mendelssohn Bartholdy) most warmly for her translations of various documents.   *J. P.*

I

THE HOMELAND OF A PRETTY GIRL

The Jeanrenauds, a family belonging to the bourgeoisie, came from Môtiers in the Val-de-Travers, in the gentle country of Neuchâtel, which, first as an earldom and subsequently as a principality, was ruled in turn by the houses of Fenis, Fribourg, Hochberg and Orléans-Longueville. These were succeeded, between 1707 and 1806, by five illustrious Kings of Prussia. Bonaparte, having stripped Frederick-William III of his sovereign rights, presented them to Berthier. But the events of 1814 were at hand and the country, regained by Prussia, became at one and the same time a principality and a Swiss canton, a curious régime which was to lead to the milk and water revolution of 1848. Since then the citizens of Neuchâtel have been Swiss! And if you told them they were Frenchmen or Prussians, they would certainly take offence. Their answer would be that it was the King of Prussia who was a Neuchâtelois and that he was so anxious to remain so that, in quite recent times, William II, fleeing to Holland, had not given up his claim on Neuchâtel and had retained it among other titles.

During the romanticist period, the capital of this remote principality had not altogether lost its mediaeval appearance. Apart from a few fine mansions bearing the coats of arms of families with names such as Chambrier, de Pierre, Montmollin, Baillod, Petitpierre, Meuron, Pury, Du Peyrou, Sandol-Roy, Bosset, Rougemont, Pourtalès or Coulon, old rustic houses huddled together, above their spacious cellars. On the hillside, watching over the castle in stormy times, a collegiate church played the rôle of a little *Notre Dame de la Garde*. For long ages this town, laved by the blue waters of the deep lake, had thrust into the clear skies of night its rusty weathervanes, its angled gables and motionless cluster of towers. For long ages, too, beneath the roofs of these houses, what a deluge of children!

An old view of the village of Travers.
By C. Calame, lith. Nicolet.
Neuchâtel Museum.

Following on each others' heels as hard as hailstones! Wives presented seventeen offspring to their husbands while the latter fought with the ... ever-victorious armies. In those days wooden bridges spanned the Seyon, the stream which, whether in spate or at low level, would hurtle through the town and—before its course was diverted—swamp the streets, the cellars and the shops, drowning rabbits and pigs, sweeping everything before it, even to the City Charter which had to be recovered by fishermen, far away downstream. Gradually, banking, paper-making and print-publishing, and, later, clock-making, and the manufacture of chocolate and cables, enabled the alert inhabitants to grow rich.

Cécile Jeanrenaud, then, was a native of this verdant principality which nestled against *la belle France*, its vine-covered slopes plunging into the emerald surface of the lake. Eventually, her own particular branch of the Jeanrenauds moved from Môtiers to the neighbouring village of Travers, with its large rectangular houses overlooking the banks of the Areuse, a stone's throw from an asphalt works exploited by wealthy silk-hatted Englishmen, who pocketed the profits leaving nothing but an impressive column of russet smoke over the country.

Originally Travers had given its name to the valley itself, where petty lordlings busied themselves, dispensing justice, safe-guarding their privileges and establishing themselves in the hierarchy of time. In 1827 their rights were handed over to the sovereign prince. As it blossomed forth, the old country-town, which had early embraced the Reformation, gradually acquired importance on the white road which, by way of Rochefort, Couvet, Môtiers and Pontarlier, led to France. Passing through this market-town, encircled by wooded slopes, terraced corn-fields and glades studded with farms, the traveller would pause at the tolling of the great bell, surprised at its solemn cathedral-like chime. Beneath the dedication engraved on it there was an ancient local name: 'Jean Regnault'.

The Val-de-Travers, the wild setting through which the slithery green stream meandered on its lazy course before rushing frantically down the gorge, was no mere strip of meadows and firs, of stones and alluvia, devoid of all civilization. Although, in order to reach it from the nearest big town or the shores of the lake, you had to ascend obliquely the slopes of the Jura, to follow the winding road from La Clusette beneath crumbling boulders, and climb up arid mountain paths in endless detours, you were at least welcomed by a valley bathed in sunshine, throbbing with life and sprinkled with villages along the main road. Wonderful lace came from workshops where women sang at their work. The building trade, precision engineering, engraving, print-publishing and the goldsmith's craft provided work enough for all. Later, watch-making gained a foothold, as did the cultivation of the sloe-berry, introduced by a certain Dr. Ordinaire; the distilled product—absinthe—was one day to be clamorously desired by the denizens of New York, Valparaiso, Melbourne, San Francisco, Aden, Shanghai and Yokohama. An extraordinary success indeed, for an Ordinary apéritif!

The ancestors of Cécile Mendelssohn Bartholdy, sojourning in Môtiers, doubtless met Rousseau and probably talked with him while he 'in order not to live like a savage', was braiding laces on a cushion, seated at the threshold of his cottage! Jean-Jacques, who, after his *Lettre sur les Spectacles* and the *Nouvelle-Héloise*, after *Emile* and the *Contrat*, had just written to the King of Prussia: 'Sire, I have spoken ill of you on many occasions, and shall most likely do so again. Nevertheless, having been expelled from France, from Geneva and from the Canton of Berne, I now come to seek refuge in your States...' Two friends of his, Isabelle d'Ivernois and Anne-Marie de Montmollin, received braided laces of his own making as wedding-presents, on condition that they breast-fed their children! I have in my possession to-day a lace, hand-woven by Rousseau himself, which he gave to Isabelle d'Ivernois, my great-great-great-grandmother.

The presence in these parts of this eccentric monomaniac attracted visitors from all four points of the compass. From Môtiers, Jean-Jacques would betake himself each week to the 'Marais', the country-house of the Sandol-Roys, near Couvet, there to wind up the clocks! It was there too that he wrote in 1765: 'On the 22nd January my book *Lettres de la Montagne* was burned at the Hague; to-day it is to be burned in Geneva; I hope it will meet with the same fate elsewhere. How strangely hot-tempered are these people in such a cold season as this! And what a lot of bonfires are lit in my honour throughout Europe! But what is the matter with my other writings, that they should have been spared? I would I had more of them worthy of being consigned to the flames!' At last, persecuted as he ever

The old Neuchâtel stage coach.
Water-colour in the possession of Mme F. Mauler-de Rutté, Neuchâtel.

was, he fled to the Ile de Saint-Pierre where, perched on a ladder, he would pluck cherries.

At the time of the Jeanrenauds the villages of the Val-de-Travers were livelier than nowadays, for a modern railway-line had not yet diverted the flow of goods and travellers. In those days there was a perpetual coming and going on the highroad from France, along which came the Dijon traffic in the shape of endless supply columns of covered waggons, led by strapping fellows in smocks of various hues, laden with wine, grain and colonial produce. The hacks, who knew every 'local' on the route, would draw up dead on time... and what could be better than a wee drop? Môtiers was an important stopping-place for post-chaises. These velvet-upholstered rattletraps were crammed full with tourists who, wedged in between fine ladies, would snatch brief glances at the countryside through the tiny glass panes. Occasionally, rounding a sharp bend, all these gentry, piled on top of one another as if in packing-cases, would overturn and pitch into the ravine.

A hundred years ago, as is well known, a few writers started the fashion of travel books. Some authors dilated tenderly on rather ugly places which they had probably never seen; while others pursued in post-chaises the celebrity guaranteed to tales told in an inn with a sprinkling of eternal snows... scribblers of every kind, who tortured their style no less than they harassed their readers. At the halts, English lords, as lean as rakes, paid stupendous prices for posies of violets, wild flowers or quaint stones. Professors at world-famous universities hatched out statistics and moral judgments while seated on an axle or enjoying a couple of boiled eggs while the horses were given their oats. Others, under the influence of a wine of unwonted potency, pencilled erratically the curves of the Jura into fiercely magnificent crags. Then, after witnessing the antics of torrents, the vine-stocks in their alignments, the gentle swell of meadows bounded by low white walls, the lakes and fir-copses, the regional costumes and the hostelries, they would observe, more surely but less contentedly, the bottom of their purses.

I should not, however, feel that I had done my duty, if I contented myself with mere anonymous references to the distinguished visitors who roamed over the homeland of the Jeanrenauds in their berlin coaches. After Rousseau, the Abbé Raynal, Sébastien Mercier, Brissot, Mirabeau, Mme de Staël, artists, poets, philosophers and other sweet-singing or gravely cogitating individuals were destined to sojourn unknowingly near their home. Sénancourt, for instance, made a pilgrimage to the Val-de-Travers just after Jean-Jacques' description of it. Mme Vigée-Lebrun, too, was enthralled by a sunset at Neuchâtel. She admired the prospect of the Alpine chain and was inspired by the Môtiers-Travers heights, which she sketched on the left whereas they stand, in fact, on the right. A Westphalian, G. B. Depping, published an account of his travels in these parts in 1812. He had his fair share of bone-shaking in carts and stage-coaches and was able to see out only on the blind side. According to him, all the roofs, towers, gables and house-fronts were adorned with tinwork that so glittered in the sunlight that one was reminded of the silver domes of Turkish mosques. Outside the post office in the capital he read a notice with the order: 'You are requested not to enter by the door, but to apply at the window.' The Post Office officials in Paris, he observes, are more accessible, for they are at home to people, whereas in Neuchâtel a clerk barely condescends to speak to you through a window-hatch. He cheered himself a little with the sight of boats sailing in with a load of plums for making tarts ready for the day of fasting, and he adds: 'The children were overjoyed at the prospect of *fasting* next day with plum-tarts nearly two-foot in diameter!'

Shelley, for his part, came from London, having abducted two young girls, one of whom, Mary Godwin, was later to become his wife. The donkey which comprised his entire retinue had already shown signs in Charenton of wishing to go no further. So, on entering the principality in August 1817, being by that time down to his last penny, Shelley precipitated himself on the nearest banker, who set him on his feet again.

Lamartine roamed over the hills where the industry of clock-making was pursued unobtrusively in secluded chalets: 'How strange it is that these hermits, for whom the passing hours record but the periodical return of the same seasons and the motionless ticking of time against the backcloth of their change-less occupations, should regulate the restless bustle of town life the world over. These inhabitants of the Jura are like the muezzins in Oriental cities, who, stationed at the summits of the minarets, suspended in mid-air, chant the hours and warn humanity below of the unsuspected flight of time as it slips by like water between men's fingers.'

From the Val-de-Travers the historian, Raoul-Rochette sent his wife a sample of lace. There Château-briand, vexed at the meagre appreciation with which his good offices were reward-ed by Louis XVIII, dreamed—forsooth ! —of becoming Go-vernor of Neuchâtel. Instead of at the pa-lace, however, he fin-ally took up residence in a lake-side hut, where his wife watch-ed a cat stealing fish from a pail of water. This same hut was

Felix Mendelssohn Bartholdy at the age of thirteen.
Sketch in the possession of M. Paul Léo, Osnabrück.

inhabited at a later date by Mme Hanska, made famous as 'L'Etrangère' by the enamoured Balzac, who came there to visit his 'beloved angel', his 'darling Eva'. A pity her confounded hus-band, M. Hanski, followed her around like a dog. 'Whenever he wasn't at his wife's skirts, he would be buttonholing me. Neu-châtel is so small a town that a woman, particularly a distinguish-ed foreign lady, cannot move one step without being noticed. As for me, I was like a cat on hot bricks.' Fenimore Cooper, who tended to miscalculate the stages of his journey, drove through

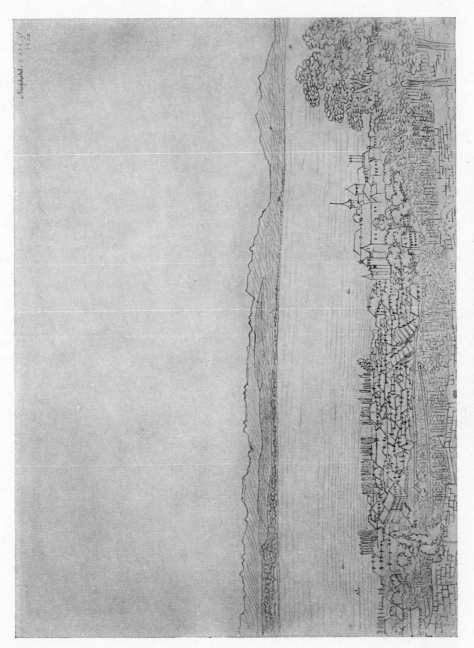

A drawing of Neuchâtel by Mendelssohn at the age of thirteen.
Page from an album in the possession of the Benecke family, Eastbourne.

the Travers gorge in the middle of a stormy night: 'I learned subsequently that we had passed like blind men by one of the most
extraordinary sights in Europe.' Proudhon, whose dissertation
on *Property* later gained him celebrity, worked as a type-setter
in a printing-works in Neuchâtel... Alexandre Dumas travelled
through the city at the time of the revolutionary fever of 1831.
Michelet was to jot down a few impressions on the place; and
Andersen, who preferred the light of day to railway tunnels and
suffered from tooth-ache, made drawings of the Col-des-Roches
and the upper reaches of the Daubs. These sketches were
published by M. Charly Guyot in his *Voyageurs romantiques
en pays neuchâtelois*.

In 1822 a child of thirteen, Felix Mendelssohn Bartholdy,
who was visiting Switzerland with his father—a wealthy Berlin
banker accompanied by his family, friends and a numerous
retinue of servants—sketched Neuchâtel in his album, as seen
from the heights overlooking the lake. The youth, his locks still
flowing about his shoulders, little knew that, fifteen years later,
he would marry a girl from those parts.

The Neuchâtelois rarely extol their own country. But when
they do embark upon the praising of its merits, or its products,
then there is nothing which can restrain them. To quote an
18th century example, François Prince, a young doctor of yeoman
stock, submitted a physico-medical paper on the subject of the
local wine to the members of Basle University. He divided his
thesis into four parts and thirty chapters. From the distinctions
he draws between red wine and white, one infers that he preferred
the former. White wine, indeed, although most wholesome in
itself, he holds to be injurious to the phlegmatic, the cachectic,
the gouty, to patients suffering from the stone and men of letters.
On the other hand, it is an excellent table wine for the obese and
people of a robust or choleric disposition! Prince calls it 'our
native nectar' and states that it quenches thirst, excites the
appetite, assists digestion, dispels obstructions and relieves ca-
tarrh. These prolegomena, packed with references to the Psalms

and the Book of Proverbs, and quotations from Horace and Voltaire, are followed by a series of notes on chylification, the strengthening of the muscles of the stomach and the elasticity of its tissues. One learns how to combat hypochondria, catarrhal fluxions, galloping consumption and breathlessness, one must drink the produce of the vine-slopes of Neuchâtel. Prince himself, so it appears, carried out exhaustive experiments: 'Anyone who enjoys a good sleep after getting drunk on this wine does not suffer from a thick head upon waking.' Finally, before this select academic gathering, he sets out thirteen questions, the last of which is a real poem in itself: 'Is truth to be found in the wine of Neuchâtel?' A student, proposing a vote of thanks in Latin verse, expresses astonishment that learning should have deserted Apollo in favour of Bacchus!

But the country is not merely a favourite growing-place of the vine with its tawny clusters: it is also the native land of the great Ostervald, the author of the famous *Catechism*, of which six thousand copies were consigned to the flames by the Parliament of Bordeaux, but of which twenty editions in various tongues nevertheless made their way all over the world. And what a vogue did his version of the Holy Bible enjoy! It was thanks to him that his native land was one day to shake itself free from the dogmatic intransigence which was beginning to overwhelm the Protestant community after it had crystallized the Gospel-truths by proclaiming, in the so-called *Consensus*, the articles of faith of the Swiss Churches. During this crisis Neuchâtel, which had remained tolerant, became the refuge of pietist émigrés. Amongst the latter came Béat-Louis de Muralt, well known for his *Lettres sur les Anglais et les Français*, which earned him the unreserved esteem of both Voltaire and Sainte-Beuve.

Having shown itself hospitable towards the victims of clerical and patrician intolerance during this episode in the time-honoured struggle between authority and freedom, the principality was later to extend a no less hearty welcome to the critics of political tyranny. For indeed, did not the Printing Association of the

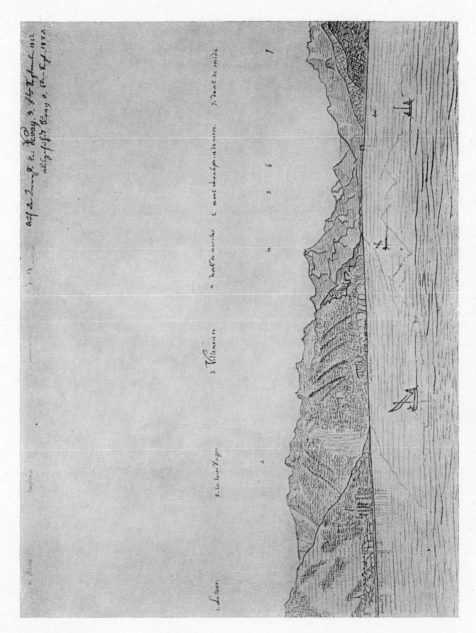

The Lake of Geneva . . . sketched by Mendelssohn at the age of thirteen.
Page from an album in the possession of the Benecke family, Eastbourne.

little capital boast Rousseau, Diderot, Baron d'Holbach and Mirabeau among its patrons? The Association's tribulations caused by the young Mirabeau are indescribably comic. Thanks to the money of a printer of Neuchâtel, the young man was enabled, in spite of the strict watch kept over him on account of previous escapades, to abduct the wife of a septuagenarian of Pontarlier. Her name was Sophie, which means 'Wisdom'! It was the printing at Neuchâtel of the *Lettres de cachet*, Mirabeau's indictment against the practice of arbitrary imprisonment at Vincennes, which provoked the intervention of Louis XVI's minister Vergennes. Frederick II intervened and Mirabeau, the future French Demosthenes, fled to Holland (with 'Wisdom' who ended up in a reformatory), but was nevertheless unable to escape being burned to death in effigy.

Much of the damage would have been avoided if foreign pamphleteers had not shown such exaggerated partiality for Swiss printers, with the result that printers of various nationalities who wished to conceal their identity felt no compunction at setting the name 'Neuchâtel' on their clandestine publications, so that the title-pages of lampoons, dubious satires and unsavoury tales, which eventually reached the four corners of the globe, were adorned in the Low Countries, Britain, France and even Rome by usurped styles. It was as if Neuchâtel, that citadel of Protestantism, had become the stronghold of innumerable rascals who straddled the printing-presses and published an unceasing torrent of politico-philosophical diatribes and pornography. During the next century the inevitable reaction set in and the strictest censorship was exercised—indeed, invoices and visiting cards alone were not subject to examination.

However, let us not forget that Cécile Mendelssohn Bartholdy, née Jeanrenaud, was to marry not a pamphleteer or a philosopher, nor a recognized writer, but a composer whose music was one day to arouse the admiration of the whole world. Naturally we ask ourselves if the people of Neuchâtel were musical and what they knew of music. Rousseau, who had a sensitive ear and who, as an amateur, had written incidental music for the *Devin du village*, which had been the wonder of all Paris in 1752, wrote tellingly on the subject of the Neuchâtelois to d'Alembert: 'They can all draw, paint and embroider a little and quite a few are musical and sing in tune.' This observation was made in the eighteenth century and it is hard to say if it was flattering or truthful. Possibly a genuine love of music already existed deep down in these people who were mainly of agricultural stock.

Rudolph of Nidau, Count of Neuchâtel, acquired some literary fame as a troubadour in the Middle Ages since his works, written in the language of the Minnesinger but Provençal in inspiration, formed a bridge between the poetry of the north and that of the Midi. But subsequently Neuchâtel heard no more than the mere echo of the choirs which were maintained, on the model of that of the Sistine Chapel, by princes, such as, for instance, Philip the Good or Charles the Bold. There was barely an instrument-maker in Neuchâtel, even before the Reformation which undermined the impetus offered by sacred music to the whole gamut of secular and drawing-room music in those countries which remained Catholic. In Germany Luther, who was an ardent admirer of the art, retained Mass in a modified form, thus leaving the way open for gigantic developments in the field of traditional religious music. In Neuchâtel, on the other hand, the Psalms of Goudimel, a Frenchman, which were chanted lifelessly in unison, were not calculated to inspire a love of composite themes, for they did not train the ear. Indeed, however valuable it may have been in other respects, the Reformation was responsible for the complete lack of folk-songs in the region.

Then again, it was the religious revolution of the sixteenth century which, by its distant repercussions, retarded the development of instrumental music. In the meantime, each man did his poor best. Mediocre violin-makers contented themselves with rough-surfaced firwood instead of the rarer species favoured by the warbling nightingale. Lusty but tuneless voices struggled with the fine art in the hope of being ready in time for the village festival and the inhabitants of Neuchâtel were accustomed to scarcely better entertainment than a catawauling street musician outside their windows. However, flute-players and pianists exercised their fingers together with the patience of their neighbours and the air vibrated with hoarse psalms, the rolling of drums, the shrilling of fifes or viols and the blare of trombones. The final touch was provided by the appearance of hosts of musical boxes—a side-line derived from clock-making. But the jingling of these whistling and singing machines was too much for even the most stoical of the Neuchâtelois, and they were hastily exported to the European courts. But by this time the more alert of the younger set were beginning to suspect that these things were perhaps ordered better elsewhere.

Such then were the first whimperings given by the musical art in its infancy at Neuchâtel, the home-town of the Jeanrenauds—who could, however, not be held responsible for any part in the business. The somewhat difficult initiation of the Neuchâtelois to music worthy of the name, was not completed until the second half of the eighteenth century, by which time operas and oratorios, orchestral suites, concertos and religious works in the grand style had already become regular features. It was, indeed, the year 1754 which saw the founding of a distinguished Academy which maintained an orchestra of professional musicians, assisted by amateurs, and which became a centre of attraction and of real culture. The Academy, though inclining to the Italian tradition, neglected neither Haydn nor Mozart and even played a little of the music of Beethoven, who was to attain such perfection in the homophonic style of instrumental composition. The high standard maintained at the twenty annual concerts redounded to the credit of this provincial capital which excelled many other Swiss cities. The Academy encouraged the development of the market for musical scores and private music libraries, in addition to inspiring teachers of music and the makers of instruments and promoting a continual and beneficial exchange of soloists.

MENDELSSOHN

3

Unfortunately, about the year 1800 the general tendency was reversed and the drama took the place of music in the affections of the Neuchâtelois. Pretty actresses captivated elderly Maecenases off-stage and they voted in favour of Marivaux rather than Mozart. This was the Academy's swan-song, after which followed thirty years of stagnation, aggravated by the Napoleonic campaigns. The Count of Escherny, who sang and played the viola, published his *Fragments sur la Musique* in Paris. Jean-Baptiste Dupuy, who was born at Corcelles, likewise deserted his native land and became musical director at the court of Prince Henry of Prussia, where, as a pupil of Fash in Berlin he perfected his talents and composed three operas.

In 1828 a gala programme performed in Neuchâtel by the *Société Helvétique de Musique* included Rossini, Haydn, Cherubini and Righini. Nevertheless, this little manifestation roused nobody from the widespread lethargy. In 1836, however, the first sacred-music choir made its appearance—a tardy offshoot of the Church choirs—and in 1858 came the reawakening and the magnificent resurgence of the art, when the vigorous *Société de Musique* was formed. This society inaugurated an annual series of symphony concerts, which were joined, from 1873 onwards, by recitals of great spiritual music given by a Choral Society. Gradually, from a musical point of view, Neuchâtel became one of the most cultured cities in Switzerland. Glancing through the programmes of excellent recitals performed there through the years, it is to be observed that the works of Mendelssohn were not overlooked. His violin concerto was performed on several occasions, as were the overtures and symphonies and the *Midsummer Night's Dream*.

And now we must consider what part was played, in this country which reared David de Purry, the great Ostervald, Abram-Louis Breguet, Pourtalès, Léopold Robert and Philippe Godet—this cradle of artists and king's tutors, this nursery of fair women—by the family of Jeanrenaud.

II

THE JEANRENAUDS

Some three centuries ago, several branches of the Jeanrenauds, striking out boldly from the original line, began to establish worthy and honourable traditions of their own in the country of Neuchâtel. Generation after generation bowed before the storm, only to spring up again as vigorous as ever. More than a few members of the family made a name for themselves, as, for example, Jeanrenaud-Besson, who was elected first to the Legislative Council and then to the Constituent Assembly of Neuchâtel, and, eventually, reached the Swiss Council of States. Marcelin, who belonged to the same federal authority, also controlled the finances of his native Canton. Paul Jeanrenaud, who followed in the footsteps of seven other members of his branch of the family who had all been Postmasters General (the precedent having been created by four brothers who enjoyed the protection of Jarry and Berthier's Council of States in 1807), became a Postmaster General in his

Coat-of-arms of the Jeanrenauds,
Postmasters General.

turn and organised the Roumanian postal services. He was, besides, president of the 4th Regional Board of the Confederacy's Mail Department. His daughter married a multi-millionaire banker from Neuchâtel who had settled in San Francisco, and this was the branch to which belonged Jeanrenaud-Racle, Postmaster in Neuchâtel from 1815 onwards—of whom mention will be made later. This line was quite separate from that of Auguste Jeanrenaud and his daughter, Cécile Mendelssohn Bartholdy.

However, even before these Jeanrenauds flourished, with their peculiar predilection for spreading tidings good or bad over the

world, others of their name had been memorable in their own way: Daniel, secretary to the Neuchâtelois guild of merchants, married the sister of Ferdinand Berthoud, clockmaker to the King of France and to his navy, member of the *Institut de France* and of the London Royal Society; another Daniel of this branch of the family (parallel to that of Cécile Mendelssohn), was preceptor at the court of Mecklenburg-Schwerin; the daughter of François Jeanrenaud-Jacot, a barrister, became Countess Miaczinsky; and Ferdinand Jeanrenaud was

Coat-of-arms of Cécile Mendelssohn's branch of the Jeanrenaud family.

an officer in the Po Volunteers, while his sister, married to a Favarger, was later to become the great-grandmother of M. Pierre Favarger, our contemporary, a former National Councillor and father of the governess to the children of the King of the Belgians.

Cécile Mendelssohn Bartholdy's ancestry can be traced as far back as Pierre Jehan Regnault, born in Travers in 1595. His son Daniel was the father of Pierre Jeanrenaud, the judge, whose wife, Esther Jeanjaquet, presented him with an heir, also named Pierre, and who became a judge of high standing himself. The latter married a Perrin-Jaquet, and his son, Frédéric Jeanrenaud-Borel, became a print-publisher at Neuchâtel.

Jeanrenaud family group.
Neuchâtel Museum.

Charles, one son of the Jeanrenaud-Borels, served as colonel of artillery under Kellermann, and another, Pierre-François, set up as a clock-manufacturer in La Chaux-de-Fonds, about the time when the town was seriously damaged by a memorable fire which destroyed sixty houses. Cécile Mendelssohn's father, Auguste Jeanrenaud, was the son of the industrialist Pierre-François and his wife, Sophie Droz, and he became a most distinguished personage, student of divinity and minister of the Reformed Church. An enamel miniature, painted under the microscope by Marie-Anne Calame of Locle, shows the mother of Sophie Droz, wearing a white bonnet with a deep blue bow under her chin and some knitting in her hands.[1] The subject of this miniature, Marie-Madeleine Droz, née Vincent, after her second marriage to a Sandoz, gave birth to a son, who became the intimate friend of the young Léopold Robert, a painter of some repute who committed suicide in Venice while he was in love with Charlotte Bonaparte.

Sophie Jeanrenaud-Droz had one brother and two sisters, one of whom, Hélène de Meuron-Droz[2], was the wife of a merchant established in La Chaux-de-Fonds, while the other, Charlotte Droz, married Jacques-François Petitpierre, a gifted preacher, dean of the Vénérable Classe from 1813 onwards and a member of the Audiences Générales. The correspondence exchanged between the two divines—the uncle, Petitpierre, and Jeanrenaud, the nephew—provides a source of precious information which enables us to gain a vivid insight into the manners and thoughts of a bygone age. Jacques-François Petitpierre, who was minister

---

[1] I published this picturesque miniature in my collection *Patrie Neuchâteloise*, vol. II, page 21, Editions de la Baconnière, Neuchâtel, 1935.

[2] François de Meuron-Droz, a merchant in the clock-making industry at La Chaux-de-Fonds, was the son of Pierre de Meuron and Rose de Luze; he had only one daughter, Hélène, who married Guillaume-Auguste d'Ivernois, son of the Chief Treasurer of the principality, in July 1808; an old document shows this wedding procession walking from the Bellevaux Manor, rue de la Pommière, to the collegiate church on the hill of the Neuchâtel castle, to the great interest of onlookers. Later the wedding party went to the house of Mme Terrisse at Saint-Blaise by means of boats and carriages. Hélène d'Ivernois-de Meuron died the following year and left no descendants.

first at Les Bayards near Les Verrières, and later at Serrières and Peseux, proved an invaluable mentor for the earnest young recruit to the clerical calling[1].

The bond of affection between the families of Droz, Jeanrenaud, Petitpierre and de Meuron was very close. During the winter in the mountains when they huddled snugly around the flickering firelight beneath the snow-burdened roofs while the howling blasts outside suggested a witches' sabbath, visits would be exchanged. They travelled up hill and down dale over silver-surfaced roads in swan-necked sledges, muffled in furs and foot-warmers, to the jingling of the sleigh-bells. And in the summer or at the time of the vine-harvesting, a hearty welcome awaited relatives who came up for the day among the lovely hills with their row upon row of vine-stocks surrounding every town and village. Plans for excursions and travels, politics and military events formed subjects for discussion in the châteaux of La Borcarderie, and Fenin, and in Le Villaret, the white mansion which surveyed the green countryside from its height, and at La Lance, an ancient abbey down by the stream, purchased by the Pourtalès from the Chevalier de Rochefort. And the ladies indulged in the latest gossip... that at Colombier, the home of Mme de Charrière (the witty Dutchwoman whose flawless French

[1] Dean Jacques-François Petitpierre-Droz, of Neuchâtel and Couvet, had, among other children, two sons: Edouard-Henri, who married into the Le Chevalier de Rochefort family, became Pastor at Dordrecht and was buried in 1827 in the cathedral of this town; and Alphonse Petitpierre, born in 1812 at Serrières, who married a Vaucher, became Pastor at Mulhouse and Saint-Aubin; he was a Neuchâtelois historian and well-known as a regional publicist; died in 1888. The latter was the father of Adolphe Petitpierre, who married at Paris, was Pastor at Corcelles, then deputy in the Grand Conseil and died at Peseux in 1907. Alphonse Petitpierre, with whom we are concerned here, was director of the Neuchâtel schools from 1864 to 1877. In 1871 he published: *Un demi-siècle de l'histoire économique de Neuchâtel*. His work: *La première académie de Neuchâtel* appeared after his death, in 1889. He was one of the founders of the *Musée Neuchâtelois* and of the *Société régionale d'histoire et d'archéologie* and lived in Neuchâtel, with his sister Julie (god-daughter and cousin of Pastor Auguste Jeanrenaud) in a house perched on the old cliffs of L'Evole; there is, among others, a pretty drawing of this primitive house which was sold to the Petitpierres by Charlotte de Chaillet d'Arnex and where Cécile Mendelssohn was to come and stay as a young girl. (I published this drawing in *Patrie Neuchâteloise*, vol. II, page 120).

I am indebted to my father, Adolphe Petitpierre, for the transmission of numerous documents which I have made use of here.

was so much admired by Mme de Staël) the servants enjoyed a
far better fare than the masters...

In 1806, the occupation of the country by the French army
of General Oudinot prompted a lively exchange of letters: one
learns that Bonaparte's soldiery pumped the wine from the
cellars as though they were man-
ning a fire-engine, but that in
grateful return they were quite
prepared to mend the breeches
of the townspeople upon whom
they were billeted.

*The unusual escutcheon of Auguste
Jeanrenaud.*
From the archives of the Bary family,
Frankfurt.

In the busy clockmaking centre which La Chaux-de-Fonds was
in those days, the watch-case
manufacturing business of Pierre-
François Jeanrenaud-Droz, in
common with other firms, was
unable to escape the ill effects
of the Napoleonic campaigns. Although his brothers-in-law did
their best to rescue him, Pierre-
François Jeanrenaud-Droz was
not able to overcome the diffi-
culties thus created until a dozen years later and with the assistance of one of his sons.

Four children were born to the Jeanrenaud-Droz: Auguste,
the theologian (in whom, as the father of Cécile Mendelssohn
Bartholdy, we are chiefly interested), was the eldest. He it was
who, in 1818, came to his father's assistance. A brother of his,
Ulysse, died early and without marrying. A sister, Caroline,
married M. Billon, and the youngest son, Pierre Jeanrenaud-
Calame, after spending some time in 1814 with the firm of Souchay in Frankfurt, became head of the Assay Office in La Chaux-
de-Fonds; he published a *Handbook of Trade* and also, in 1842,
a *Table of Gold and Silver Coinages.*

And now let us take leave of the rest of the family to follow in his career one of its members who, stimulated by a simple faith and a high-minded and cheerful disposition, felt the call to Holy Orders.

Auguste Jeanrenaud, 1788—1819.

Pastor at Frankfurt, father of Cécile Mendelssohn Bartholdy.
Pen-and-ink drawing in the possession of Jacques Petitpierre.

III

A DISTINGUISHED PROTESTANT

The life of Auguste Jeanrenaud, the father of Cécile Mendelssohn Bartholdy, cut off in its prime, was so brief that his biographer, besides emphasising conspicuous events in his career, is bound to touch upon less important details.

It was surely only fitting that a theological student should start by playing all sorts of pranks. For instance, he wrote from Basle in 1804: 'My room looks out on to the pig-market, and every Friday fifteen to twenty dealers, together with two to three hundred charming squealing animals, foregather outside my window. As this annoys me intensely I attempt to revenge myself like this: our house was formerly a Carmelite convent, an ancient, large, broad-fronted building with small windows, overlooking the square on three sides. Each time they strike a bargain, the dealers summon the market overseer by giving a whistle and shouting: Pshaw! at the tops of their voices. The overseer, being a short thick-set little man with a limp in both legs, moves about only with the greatest difficulty, particularly in the midst of a crowd, nearly knocking down at least two people at every step. Now I have a whistle which gives a perfect imitation of that of the dealers, and so, passing along from one end of the house to the other, I put my head to the window-bars, uttering that tiresome "pshaw". You should just see my little man then, getting all hot and bothered ... by the time he reaches the place from which he thinks the call came all he can do is to open wide eyes and a gaping mouth...' Did Mendelssohn ever hear this story? Doubtless he would have been amused by these concerts in the market-square at Basle, where the orchestra was seconded by an amateur who was later to become the father of his wife[1].

Jeanrenaud, meanwhile, had settled down to his divinity studies. The year 1806 saw the re-establishment in Neuchâtel of a society where candidates for the ministry would discuss plans for sermons and practise preaching. The meetings were attended by the town councillors. There, two preachers of repute, de Bellefontaine and Chaillet, began taking an interest in young Jeanrenaud. Chaillet, whose cheerful and ruddy features betokened a fundamentally kindly nature, was a professor and literary critic, a contributor to the *Journal Helvétique* and a friend of Mme de Charrière, who died recently; he was to exercise a most happy influence over the young man. The instruction was carried on with zest: 'M. Chaillet told us to recite the beginning of the first funeral oration of Bossuet. We took turns to stand in the middle of the room, behind a chair, but we all gave a very poor performance; certainly it is extremely difficult to do justice to this exordium. Nevertheless, our colleague Perrot was hissed ... Continually gazing up in the air as if he were talking to the birds, with his angry and monotonous voice and his perpetual fidgeting with his hands and feet, he created a most disagreeable impression on his audience. And yet, so he told us, he had rehearsed this piece several times before his mother.' Arduous indeed was this training by the light of the orations of the Bishop of Meaux!

These were the times when people used to write memoranda on the backs of playing-cards (even using them for signing receipts and powers of attorney). A microscope is needed to read Chaillet's sermons which were jotted down in this way.

---

[1] Rudolf Wackernagel, a historian born in Basle, published a report on this building, which was an abandoned convent built on the site of the present Casino, composed of small houses built on to the walls in the style of monasteries, and which, after sheltering Jeanrenaud, who lodged with M. Baillif, served as a home for illegitimate children, and as an asylum, and was finally demolished in 1843. This edifice was joined to the Barfüsser-Kirche, to-day a History Museum, which was next to a cloister of which there are some curious water-colours. Plans show this pig-market when it had become an elegant square, which is still called the 'Sauplatz' or 'Saibi' by the people of Basle!

Incidentally, a minister once, to the dismay of his congregation, threw down in a sweeping gesture from the pulpit a pack of cards containing the whole of his peroration.

During the previous century there had developed a schism which was unique in history, when some people put their faith in God's never-failing mercy and others believed in eternal damnation. The country was divided into two factions, those in favour of Hell, and those against it. Frederick II, when approached on the subject, rolled his large eyes under his three-cornered hat and informed his audience that if the Neuchâtelois were so keen on being eternally damned he certainly had no objection. Jeanrenaud was witness to some fine tirades, for this is how he commented on some lapses from decorous behaviour: 'M. le Pasteur Touchon is in very bad odour, and this ill-feeling is the result of his having been the first to cry "Long Live the Emperor!" from the pulpit, on the very day of the transfer of sovereignty.' For it was indeed at this time that the principality passed like a basket of fruit from the grasp of the King of Prussia to the fair hands of France. Fair hands—well, perhaps. But the burden of occupation charges was a crushing one. Jeanrenaud's blood boiled whenever he saw women and girls of all classes rushing to dance at M. Bovet's in Areuse, where the terrace was always packed with soldiers. And he was aghast that a woman called Steck—the elderly wife of a miller at Boudry—offered 40 louis to any man willing to take the place of the most repulsive and profligate grenadier in the company stationed at Auvernier, who had been her lover. In the peaceful fishing village of Auvernier the young student lived opposite M. Gaullieur, whose son, in partnership with Sainte-Beuve, later published in the *Revue des Deux Mondes* and the *Revue Suisse* selected extracts from the correspondence between Benjamin Constant and Mme de Charrière, the latter being as yet unknown to the general public. Jeanrenaud remarks that one Neuchâteloise, at least, preferred the company of a fellow-countryman to that of the vulgar soldiery from over the border, but he cannot forbear to criticise the relationship between Gaullieur Senior and Henriette L'Hardy, a former lady-in-waiting to the Countess of Doenhof, and third morganatic wife of Frederick William II: 'Philosophy is always leading people astray: we have with us here in Auvernier Mlle Henriette L'Hardy, a pseudo-philosopher and a keen disciple of Mme de Charrière, and whom I see every day coming out to meet her lover, M. Gaullieur. She is absolutely crazy about him, as I infer from what happens every evening under my very window. All this can only end badly.' These words were perhaps prophetic, for two years later Henriette L'Hardy, who had married in the meantime, died in giving birth to the writer Gaullieur.

But let us return to the study of Massillon and Bossuet, and of such questions as whether the Reformation would withstand the onslaught of Socinianism, then in such vogue in the city of Calvin. Meantime, in Neuchâtel Oudinot was cursing the knave who was spreading confusion throughout the principality by proclaiming that Berthier would become King of Switzerland, and Jeanrenaud had moved to Geneva. There, the young divine, whose correspondence already revealed a remarkably mature outlook, struck up a friendship with J.-E. Cellérier, a future Rector of the Academy and President of the Church sessions. And this is what he wrote of the town which had just been reunited with France and whose Church had been disestablished and of his teachers there: '. . . they (the professors) are decent enough, but mostly rather boring. M. Picot, whose good humour seems to be inexhaustible, keeps up a running commentary on the latest political events for the benefit of the students, who take good care to remind him that time is up whenever the bell rings. M. Pasteur, who wears a wig of flaxen hair and teaches patristics in execrable French, is the most stupid man I know. M. Duby enjoys a well-deserved reputation, although his originality chiefly consists in interlarding Claparède with endless quotations.' Decidedly the Pasteurs, father and son, did small credit to their name: 'I listened this morning to a sermon by M. Pasteur, son of the professor, who is as much a disgrace to the

Church as his father is a disgrace to the Faculty. His discourse was all about polytheism, polygamy and the customs of Haiti and Cuba ... it was sheer vulgarity, false sentiment and ridiculous bombast.' This was merely the verdict of a student, of course, but through it can be glimpsed a regret for the austere restraints and severe discipline in teaching and in practice which were now a thing of the past. One must remember too that Geneva was the happy hunting ground of a number of Methodist leaders who were more at home in a drawing room than a Cathedral, and that there was a saying, around 1840, that 'Every man is a Church unto himself'.

Disappointed, Jeanrenaud returned to Neuchâtel, there to await the day of his consecration. Nowadays the laying on of hands is a public ceremony which is held in Church and repeated separately for each candidate; but in 1808 Jeanrenaud and his companions were called to the Holy Ministry all together, in conclave. Candidates had to be at least seventeen years old and to have studied five years and secured the acceptance of fifteen 'propositions'; they had also to have abstained from worldy pleasures and Freemasonry; further, it was necessary that their signatures should be appended to the text in Latin (or in French as from 1821) of the *Consensus Helveticus*, which had been tacitly, though not formally, accepted by the Church of Neuchâtel. There was an obligation to support the views of a brother-minister, except where the harmony of the Reformed faith might be prejudiced. The oath taken by Jeanrenaud and his friends was 'to further the honour and glory of God, and to dedicate our lives to this task ... We solemnly promise to eschew schism, dissensions and plots, and, if need be, to sacrifice our persons and our possessions in defence of God's Word'. It was, indeed, no small thing to be received into the ecclesiastical aristocracy of the Vénérable Classe[1].

---

[1] On the 18th May, 1808, Jeanrenaud's fellow-candidates for consecration at Neuchâtel were Frédéric-Louis Herzel, later minister at Sornetan, Jean-Alphonse Franel, later at Travers, Bevaix and Boudry, Jean-Georges Schlenker, a native of Würtemberg, who died in Holland, young Auguste Touchon (son of the minister Frédéric Touchon at La Chaux-de-Fonds), minister

In 1810, after having filled a number of interim vacancies, Jeanrenaud was elected minister of the French Church in Frankfurt by eighteen votes to the seventeen cast in favour of the young cleric Paul Appia. It is strange how a man's fate—and, in this case, Mendelssohn's own destiny was already concerned—hangs by a thread! In this town, or, more precisely, in Bockenheim, a Calvinist parish existed which had been founded as far back as 1554 by Valerand Poulain, a zealous preacher whom Calvin described as a muddle-head! The arrival of many refugees at the time of Philip II and, later, after the revocation of the Edict of Nantes, had swollen the numbers of this French-speaking community. In 1790 in a fine grove known as L'Allée a chapel was built in the Louis XVI style and this can still be seen at No. 7 Goetheplatz. This chapel plays an important part in the present story. As the ringing of bells was forbidden to all other denominations but the officially recognised Catholic and Lutheran, the absence of tower or bell-turret gave it, like certain other religious buildings, the appearance of a private mansion.

Prince Carl Theodor von Dalberg.

at Lyons and afterwards at Hanau, who became an intimate friend of Jeanrenaud and later gave an account of the latter's death in a letter to Mme de Sandol-Roy at Darmstadt. In the batch also was Paul-Frédéric Penneveyre, a Vaudois, who, at the time of his death in 1842 was minister in New York. The Dean in charge, Samuel-David Bonhôte, minister at Boudry, presided at the ceremony. The Salle du Conclave was on the site of what is now the Salle du Grand Conseil of the little republic of Neuchâtel.

Jeanrenaud's nomination had been no simple matter. Frankfurt had forfeited its independence on becoming the capital of a Grand Duchy in 1806, and Church matters henceforth depended on the goodwill of His Highness Carl Dalberg, Prince Primate and Elector of Mainz—a sort of overlord of the Rhine Confederation for whom Napoleon had warily appointed a successor in the person of Eugène de Beauharnais. But an ancient episcopal law also recognised the competence of the Senate in such matters. Who, therefore, was to ratify Jeanrenaud's appointment and his admission to the freedom of the City ? In fact this responsibility fell to Prince Dalberg after consultations between Councillor von Seeger and Baron d'Eberstein.

Jean-Daniel Souchay.
Pastor at Frankfurt.

Jeanrenaud was assistant to M. Souchay, a surly old minister with an aquiline nose, who taxed the young man with ignoring 'the dignified style' and became vastly incensed when he began to notice hosts of carriages which he had never seen before all drawn up at the door of his chapel. Jeanrenaud attempted to find a refuge from his colleague's taunts in the sermons of the famous Chaillet, which had just been published, and in the preparation of his own addresses for the winter; the approach of this season filled him with misgivings for in those times fashionable Frankfurt society indulged in 'such extravagant dinners and suppers that every year the advent of spring heralded the death through indigestion of at least a hundred persons'. We learn that there were many wealthy people among the congregation and that the poor were provided for with generosity. Ostentatious in their wealth, the bourgeois families aped the nobility, and there were trade fairs organised on an extremely lavish scale. Then, at the end of October 1810, conditions began to deteriorate. 'The townspeople are full of consternation. A French regiment has arrived, together with two battalions who are in control of the city gates. The general in command of all this rabble informed the merchants immediately that they would have to declare their stock of English wares and colonial produce. The former were to be confiscated while the latter would be subjected to a 50% tax. This spells the ruin of the entire trading community.'

Jeanrenaud had to pay his respects to the Prince Primate who spent a few weeks in Frankfurt from time to time. He was on excellent terms with His Highness right from the start.

The minister from Neuchâtel felt a little homesick amid the vicissitudes of the occupation, remembering the picturesque manse at Les Bayards, its cosy library and the 'dining-room where we used to sip our white 1804 wines and our tawny 1802's with so much happiness'. (This was an echo, after seventy years, of the eulogies of a certain *Docteur Prince!*)

Old Souchay, thinking that his colleague, a tall handsome man with a commanding and resolute bearing, would take a fancy to one of the more charming young ladies of Frankfurt, asked him one day: 'Pretty girls in the congregation?' 'I saw only your granddaughter', was the reply. Elisabeth-Wilhelmine Souchay was a child of fourteen. As a matter of fact Jeanrenaud wrote to Serrières: 'I should be tempted to say with La Fontaine: *J'ai vu beaucoup d'hymens, aucun d'eux ne me tente,* if that were not a little impolite. Marriage was no part of my plans when I came here. A wife would not want to leave her parents and would be even less willing to settle down in the Val-de-Ruz or the Val-de-Travers. I do not know how it is, but ever since my last passion in Neuchâtel any sort of tender sentiment has been so alien to me that it would really be a miracle if I were to fall in love again ...' Doubtless this was no more than one of the usual cases of disappointed young love.

In 1811 Jeanrenaud presided at the funeral of his old colleague, Souchay. In his oration at the funeral of the dead man 'who was very passionate both in good and evil', Jeanrenaud 'chose to emphasise the part played by the love of God as the moving principle of all his actions'. Taking leave of his hostess, Mme de Neufville, he moved into the twelve pleasant and richly appointed rooms which made up the minister's apartments and which were situated above the chapel. But it is a fact that for some time previously he had by reason of his culture, integrity and energy, and his commanding personality, been regarded as the true head of this huge parish belonging to the Waldensian sect.

On his way to Lyons he spent some time in Neuchâtel and Geneva, where, once again, his impression of the ecclesiastical circles was most depressing. In spite of the fact that the increase in immorality caused by the Napoleonic Wars should have encouraged Christians to close their ranks and that, in effect, in many places Calvinists, Waldensians and Lutherans were holding joint prayer meetings and celebrating the Lord's Supper together with the hope that they might all become united under the common banner of an 'Evangelical Church' ... nevertheless, 'the continual petty squabbles of the Genevese are most unseemly and I have but little patience with them. What infuriates me is that I am persuaded that love of truth and religion play no part in all this chicanery but merely serve as a cloak for the immeasurable vanity of this little people and for the presumptuousness which marks out the great majority of its ministers. It was vanity which prompted Malan and his associates to adopt a rigid and intolerant Calvinism; again, it was vanity that drove Chenevière and his friends to muzzle their opponents who accused them of rejecting orthodoxy only because they did not understand it and had never even meditated upon its doctrines much less grasped them thoroughly. A Genevan cannot forgive anyone who accuses him of ignorance or want of intelligence; call him a rogue or a knave and he will remain calm, but a hint that he is lacking in brains or learning and he will fly into a rage.' Jeanrenaud confides further in his uncle on the subject of Malan and Chenevière[1]: 'Malan is consumed by a thirst for celebrity. As for Chenevière, whose knowledge and capacity are scarcely more than mediocre, his pretensions are boundless. His satisfaction at enumerating, in a letter I have before me, every single occasion when he was able to display courage, wisdom and forethought, is something positively unique.'

Pastor Jeanrenaud deplored the ill effects of these continual dissensions on points of theology. The French Protestants were appalled at the humiliating controversies which made them the laughing stock of the Catholics and Jeanrenaud, as an impartial observer, was heart-broken to see strong religious convictions vitiated by theological hair-splitting. He was alarmed by the danger of new schisms which were threatening to divide the Protestants at the time of the Réveil (the famous movement of the early 19th century known among historians as the *Réveil franco-suisse*). One wonders what he would have thought, had he lived longer, of the religious movement which some people have accused of being nothing but the transposition of Romanticism into the field of religion. Would he have continued in his condemnation of men such as Vinet, Monod, Merle d'Aubigné, Eugène Bersier, Pressensé, Godet, Secrétan—all of whom played notable parts in the Evangelical movement? Nothing seems less certain... His correspondence is, in fact, made up of discreet confidences between ministers, and it gives a fairly exact picture of the general atmosphere and prevailing conditions at that time.

---

[1] Abraham-César Malan embraced the theories of the Réveil with enthusiasm at Geneva; he substituted Bible-study for the teaching of the catechism in his lessons; he built a chapel, *l'Eglise du Témoignage*, and published the *Chants de Sion*. Jean-Jacques-Caton Chenevière, doctor and professor of theology, was several times rector of the *Académie de Genève*. He was the author of *Essais théologiques*, of *Sermons*, and of six volumes of *Dogmatique chrétienne*.

In writing to his uncle in Serrières on the subject of the preachers of Neuchâtel[1] he frequently emphasised the extreme difficulty of the art of preaching: 'It is terribly hard to preach well. I am, perhaps, inclined to judge my fellow-preachers rather harshly, but I find it just as easy to find fault with myself: out of thirty-two sermons I have fathered I am painfully aware that barely five or six deserve attention.'

Elisabeth Jeanrenaud-Souchay, 1796—1871.
Girardet Miniature in the possession of Mme Deluz-de Bary, Areuse.

The letters of Cécile Mendelssohn Bartholdy's father-to-be merit closer study. They are full of penetrating observations on the habits and outlook of the respectable bourgeoisie of those times, and provide a more characteristic picture of the period than certain uninspiring accounts of court events and other such formalities.

While he was still a bachelor and imagined that he would leave no heirs, he wrote in touching terms to his aunt Charlotte Petitpierre, suggesting that, in memory of him, she should add the name of Auguste to that of Alphonse which she had just

---

[1] Jeanrenaud exchanged letters with Claude de Perrot, Berthoud, Du Pasquier, Bonhôte and César-Henri Monvert, all pastors of Neuchâtel. He finds Perrot's emotionalism wearisome. 'Henriod, no matter what his father and M. le Ministre Du Pasquier say, will never be anything but a dull preacher. He has neither fire nor vigour; to my mind he is the second volume of Gagnebin and not at all of Courvoisier, as people try to make out.'

Jeanne Souchay de la Duboissière.
A distant forbear of Cécile Jeanrenaud.
Painted in Geneva in 1680. Property of the Souchays, Marburg.

given to her latest-born, the future historian. This letter, which left Frankfurt by post-chaise on the same day that the christening took place, arrived too late. So there was to be no Alphonse-Auguste! The godparents, who had been chosen long before, were Alphonse de Sandoz-Rollin of the Château of Beauregard, an ex-*Conseiller d'Etat*, and his wife, née Caroline de Chambrier. It was this same Alphonse Petitpierre who was later to sort out and file Jeanrenaud's letters in the family archives, thus facilitating the task of his grandson in writing the present work.

At a time when Jeanrenaud had no idea of marrying, a friendship, platonic at first, sprang up between him and, surprisingly enough, the granddaughter of the man concerning whom he had so recently commented: 'Passionate in good and evil things, he did all for God!' [1] It seems that a common admiration for sermons full of fire and soaring eloquence gradually developed into mutual love, consideration and esteem. Mlle Souchay was still playing with her dolls and it was in her doll-cupboard that she kept her letters. Young girls were married at a very early age in those days ... if they married at all! and so an engagement was arranged and approved by her parents. In the meantime Elisabeth, aged fifteen, was allowed to correspond with her fiancé. She completed her education by travelling, with relations and friends, and spent over a year in Italy. 'Every day', wrote Jeanrenaud to Neuchâtel, 'I am more delighted by my future wife, who is a marvel of vivacity and tenderness. Mlle Souchay, from whom I have received ten pages written in Florence, is

---

[1] One must not misjudge Jean-Daniel Souchay, who was a most distinguished minister. In the unpublished pages of her diary, which she wrote in 1867 at the age of seventy, his grand-daughter Elisabeth observes, indicating that she is quoting a third person: 'M. le pasteur Souchay was a warm-hearted man, full of faith and piety, frank almost to the point of bluntness. Sometimes his zeal led him into the error of becoming prejudiced about people, but his memory is blessed because he was truly and sincerely attached to his parishioners. During a disastrous period of sophistry and revolution he upheld the respect of religion and the pastor's duties in his church at Frankfurt. He apostrophised persons of every rank and age with great spirit, and this made him feared, but his charity, his piety, his integrity and his eagerness to be of service made him beloved. It is obvious that his ministry had God's blessing and one can notice particularly the veneration in which he was held by his catechumens.'

now in Naples with her caravan.' The wedding was celebrated on the 3rd January, 1814.

Now that we know who the Jeanrenauds were, let us consider the origins of the Souchays, who began to play a part in composing the *milieu* from which Mendelssohn chose his own wife. They were a Huguenot family who came from the Loiret. Daniel Souchay de la Duboissière and Jeanne de Bêne, born at Gien, took refuge in Geneva towards the end of the 17th century. Their descendants settled in Hanau and later in Frankfurt. Jeanrenaud's father-in-law was a man of great wealth, an importer of colonial produce with warehouses in Frankfurt, Milan, London and Manchester. His firm, which traded first in Italy under the name of Mylius, was afterwards known as Souchay & Perret, and then as C. C. Souchay, when Perret [1], an astute but over-speculative business-man, was restricted to representing his partner in London. The powerful house of Souchay, besides trading in manufactured goods, also had a banking department which carried out important transactions in St. Petersburg, Egypt and Asia. Carl-Cornelius Souchay—the father of Senator

---

[1] François Perret, the partner of C. C. Souchay, was the only son of the banker, Jean-Jacques Perret, who married, in 1752, Suzanne Behaghel, sister-in-law of the Würtemberg councillor Sillereissen, of Stuttgart, who died a colonel in Russia, in 1777. François Perret's sister, Jeanne-Marie, married François Johannot, son of a paper-merchant at Annonay; after this marriage Jean-Jacques Perret put a large amount of money into a new company at Lyons, J. J. Perret, François Johannot & Cie.

Jean-Jacques Perret was the son of Pierre-Abram Perret, of Grandson, on Neuchâtel Lake, and, after his own marriage in 1716 to the daughter of a wealthy silk merchant, Sara-Maria Heldevier, of Frankfurt, he settled in this town. The Perrets invested large sums in the silk-works of Johannot, Levrat & Cie. in Lyons, and in the paper-works of Mathieu, Johannot & Fils, in the glass-works of Rives-de-Gier and in the Frankental, Broignard & Cie. and Harscher & Cie. banks.

François Perret was considered by his partner, C. C. Souchay, to be an imprudent speculator; Souchay broke up the partnership with him in 1811, retaining him only as his representative in London. François Perret lived in London and Frankfurt where he still owned a house in the Marché aux Chevaux (No. 10) in 1849.

The Souchays and the Perrets were not related. The partnership was the result of their being on excellent terms and owning two large adjoining houses on the Mein, near the Fahrthor, with entrances in the Altemainzergasse. This is an interesting detail because it was in one of these houses — that belonging to the Souchays, rebuilt, and called the *Fahrthor*, that Mendelssohn was married in 1837. Here, too, Cécile Mendelssohn died, in 1853.

Souchay, who was an eminent character in Frankfurt and after whom one of the city's thoroughfares was named—began by finding niches for his sons in the London and Manchester offices, and then married his daughter off to the minister of the Church to which he and his wife, née Schunck[1] ,were both deeply attached.

The portraits given here of Pastor Jeanrenaud and his fiancée appear to have been done at the same time. That of Jeanrenaud, of which there are three originals, was painted by an unknown master, but the miniature showing Elisabeth Souchay is signed 'Girardet'. This was possibly the celebrated artist who illustrated Jean Hubner's *Histoire de la Bible* and who was well-known in Paris for the great success of his etchings on the Revolution and also of those for the Musée de Napoléon. A visit from the Emperor Alexander, his illustrations for La Fontaine's Fables, and his portraits of the Kings of Prussia and many other celebrities of the time, all helped to establish his reputation. He was an unlucky eccentric, and, as a result of the blockade of the Continent and other troubles of that period, he received a letter from an Englishwoman accepting his proposal

---

[1] *The Schunck Family*. The wife of Carl-Cornélius Souchay, grandmother of Cécile Mendelssohn Bartholdy, was Hélène-Elisabeth Schunck. The Schuncks came from the Low Countries at the time of the Spanish rule. Johann-Nathanel von Schunck was raised to noble rank in 1715 and became a baron in 1719. The German branch of the Schuncks or von Schuncks of Hanau are descended from him and his wife Anne-Marie von Schütz; their grandson, Major Johann-Carl Schunck, who married Wilhelmine-Christine Hartmann, daughter of the Pastor of Windecken (great-grandmother of Cécile Mendelssohn Bartholdy), lived in Schluchtern-Hanau. It was at Windecken that the daughter of Major Schunck, Hélène-Elisabeth, married Carl-Cornélius Souchay. The Schuncks were officers, civil servants, or followed the liberal professions. After the Souchay-Schunck marriage, several Schuncks went into business. The firm of Schunck-Souchay & Cie. in Manchester, which handled woollens and velvets, was a feeler for the great intercontinental enterprise of Carl-Cornélius Souchay. The Schuncks were related to the Beneckes, an excellent Protestant family, which came from Silesia, also concerned in the same line of business as the Myliuses of Frankfurt, Milan and England. Marie Mendelssohn, the composer's daughter, was later to marry another member of this family, Victor Benecke, of London, whose son, one of our contemporaries, Mr Paul Benecke, is to-day a professor at Oxford University. Henriette Benecke, née Souchay, sister-in-law of Pastor Auguste Jeanrenaud-Souchay, left for the use of his relations *Alte Geschichten*, a private collection, published in Germany and incorporated in 1933, in English, in *The von Schunck Family*, a work, not for sale, with a genealogical table, by Sir John Edward Darnton.

of marriage only twenty-five years after his offer had been made. He was a man with a chaste, even prudish outlook: neither his visits to the Italian museums with their myriads of nudes, nor

Hélène-Elisabeth Souchay née *Schunck, 1774—1851.*
Oil-painting by Carl-Joseph Stieler,
in the possession of Mme de Coulon-Jeanrenaud, Miltenberg Château.

Paris with its licentious pictures, where Morality, all too lightly clad, discarded its last veil with easy-going regularity, ever persuaded him to represent a female whose leg could be seen above the garter. Abraham Girardet, however, was the eldest of four brothers, all of them artists; one, whose name was Abraham-Louis, had travelled a great deal and spent some time

Carl-Cornélius Souchay, merchant, 1768—1835.
Oil-painting by Carl-Joseph Stieler, in the possession of Mme de Coulon-Jeanrenaud,
Miltenberg Château.

in Germany. He, too, did some very fine miniatures and was an artist of some repute, so it is perhaps more likely that it was he who painted Elisabeth Souchay.

The unsigned pen-and-ink portrait of her husband was probably the work of the Swiss water-colourist, Gabriel Lory, who knew him well. The sketch is adorned with a triple-spired church, a freakish edifice, the like of which has never been seen either in Frankfurt or Neuchâtel, or even in Lyons or Avignon or any other town with which Jeanrenaud was associated. The explanation of this seemingly unexpected background was that it symbolises a spiritual coat-of-arms and suggests the Fabric, in the ecclesiastical sense of the term; it is intended to flatter Jeanrenaud, whose Frankfurt chapel, dedicated to an unrecognised religion, was permitted neither a fine avenue of trees, nor a tower nor bell-ringing.

A correspondence sparkling with witty gossip was exchanged over a number of years by Jeanrenaud and a charming and most distinguished friend of his, Mme de Sandol-Roy, the brilliant English wife of Colonel François de Sandol-Roy, who served in the pay of England in India, with the Neuchâtelois regiment of the Comte de Meuron. Sandol, who in 1815 had been attached to the staff of General Bachmann, commander-in-chief of the Swiss army during the Hundred Days, had become friendly with Jeanrenaud when he was a student in Neuchâtel and entertained him occasionally in his vast mansion overlooking the Place du Nouvel Hotel-de-Ville [1].

When Henri de Sandol-Roy, the colonel's son, came to stay

---

[1] Among the Sandol-Roys, who came from Locle and were an aristocratic Neuchâtelois family, were officers in the service of France, mayors, a *Conseiller d'Etat*, and generals in the service of Holland. They were connected with the Gingins, barons of La Sarraz, with the Le Chevaliers of Rochefort, with a branch of the Roys of Val-de-Travers, which died out and whose name remained to them by a special authorisation of the Prussian Government. They were also connected with the van Schoors, Barwells, with the Counts van den Bosch, or the Barons de Chambrier. They lived during the winter in a fine house at Neuchâtel, still standing at the corner of the Terreaux and the Faubourg de l'Hôpital. They lived in the summer time at the 'Marais' near Couvet, the country house celebrated by the poetess Alice de Chambrier. This property which was formerly occupied by high society and officers taking a rest in the country, belongs to the descendants of the Sandol-Roys to-day. Colonel François de Sandol-Roy, married to a Barwell, built himself another house at Neuchâtel, on the Promenade du Faubourg; his wife went to Paris with the Countess de Pourtalès-Castellane, to choose furniture worthy of this house, which is now No. 56, Faubourg de l'Hôpital.

in Frankfurt, Jeanrenaud was his religious instructor and welcomed him frequently at his home, together with other young
Neuchâtelois pupils of the select Institut Hofmann at Rœdel-
heim. This establishment, situated on the outskirts of Frankfurt,
specialised in the instruction of young men in languages, music,
etiquette, dancing and riding. In 1813 it was ransacked by the
Cossacks who left only the walls standing. Hofmann, with his
little band of budding aristocrats, sought safety within the town.
Meanwhile, on the Mein Bridge, Frenchmen and Bavarians were
exchanging a lively fusillade: 'Every house is chock-full of
soldiers', wrote Jeanrenaud. 'I, myself, have ten of them billeted
on me, most of these belonging to the Russian Guard.' His
brother, Pierre, who was staying with him at the time, re-
ported in November of the same year: 'The Emperors of Russia
and Austria have just arrived here and the latter has received
the honours due to the supreme head of the German Empire.'
Jeanrenaud was present at the ceremony with the Protestant
clergy.

In the following year an outbreak of influenza took heavy
toll of civilians and soldiers alike. Colonel Charles Jeanrenaud,
the minister's uncle, who served under General Kellermann,
returned from Russia, where he had endured terrible sufferings:
two horses were killed under him, a cannon-ball stripping the
flesh from his left side; afterwards, in order not to freeze on
horseback, he was obliged to cover a hundred leagues on foot
with a raging fever. When the Cossacks eventually released him,
after robbing him of his entire savings consisting of seventy louis
d'or, he was a mere skeleton. Mme de Sandol-Roy received from
her friend news of the Neuchâtel Battalion raised by Berthier,
the so-called 'bataillon des Canaris', which had been absorbed
into the Imperial Guard: immediately before the Battle of
Hanau it marched, exhausted, through Frankfurt. M. de Gorgier,
who intended to re-form the unit in Posen, commented: 'I have
seen all the officers of the battalion except the captains; it is a
well-composed body of troops. Most of them, however, still need

a little instruction and discipline, which they will soon acquire if their training is pursued in Berlin. There is still a fairly high proportion of deserters.'

Overworked and worn out by thousands of visits to military hospitals, Jeanrenaud had a nervous breakdown, from which he recovered only with difficulty. At his house there was an endless procession of people begging favours. Men like de Pourtalès, Paul and Frédéric Du Pasquier, General de Sandol-Roy, Charles de Perregaux, another Neuchâtelois who had volunteered to fight for France and was also to become a general, Bedaulx-de-Luze, with his 'weakness for principalities', Morel, Droz, Jeanjaquet, Brun, who was arrested in Strasbourg after an escapade, and 'that hare-brained Pury', not to mention countless parishioners and callers, were always assured of finding open house and a friendly welcome at the presbytery.

In 1814, twelve months after the Battle of Leipzig, lost by the French who were betrayed by the Saxons, the anniversary was celebrated with great festivities by the people of Frankfurt. The bells rang out all over the town for an hour and in the middle of a square of troops a tent was set up where the clergy of various faiths celebrated divine service. To the sound of incessant gun salvoes, the youth of the city danced round the public squares or sang hymns in the towers, to the accompaniment of wind instruments. In the evening a display of illuminations and fireworks was given.

The weight of the burden on Pastor Jeanrenaud's shoulders grew ever heavier in those troubled days, and as he was working desperately hard he hoped some young Probationer might be appointed to assist him in his task. Three candidates for the post—one of whom was his friend Edouard Diodati, who later became professor and librarian in Geneva and was the author of an *Essai sur le Christianisme* 'literally persecuted me with testimonials', we learn from a letter written to Dean Petitpierre, his uncle, soon after the latter had received the King of Prussia at Neuchâtel. He also adds: 'Mercier has sent me the text of the prayer composed and read out by you on the occasion of the King's visit [1]'.

In 1815 Jeanrenaud, who continued to work harder and harder, began to suffer from an alarming cough, but this, though it seemed as if it would become very serious, was alleviated to some extent thanks to the loving care of his wife, the mother of his son Charles. At this time events were proving very surprising: Napoleon's return in March, like a bolt from the blue, took Europe unawares—'and particularly our German friends who were busily and greedily sharing out their spoils.' Jeanrenaud observes that 'people here believe there will be another war, more terrible than the first, which will be followed by the disruption of France. What I find hardest to forgive is that Bonaparte's expedition has prevented the one I had promised myself I would make to Serrières this summer.' That same year, after the final overthrow of the Emperor, Frankfurt became the seat of the German Diet, regained its status as a Free City and acquired a democratic constitution.

Amid the hurly-burly of these dramatic events which were changing the face of the world and stirring men to sacrifices of all kinds, the work of the parish was making sure progress and Jeanrenaud continued in his care of his protégés: for instance, in order to keep young Henri de Sandol away from the dangers of 'all sorts of doubtful women at the theatre' he invited him to the Souchay's private box. Sandol later decided to join the army in his turn. His mother, who had a very strong English accent, nevertheless managed to pick up a few expressive French phrases

---

[1] When the Principality of Neuchâtel was taken from the French by the Prussians, the Dean Jacques-François Petitpierre officiated at divine service on the 14th July 1814. A Te Deum was sung in honour of Frederick William II in the collegiate church. The King, moved, embraced Petitpierre when he left the pulpit. The prince, who came to the country with his cousin Frederick of Orange in 1819 and attended a service at the chapel of La Chaux-de-Fonds, raised his glass in honour of this same Dean at a luncheon, and thanked him for the great welcome he had given him. Jacques-François Petitpierre had a remarkable talent for preaching. He was decorated with the Ordre du Lys by Louis XVIII, as were several members of his family, and he died in 1819, a short time after his reception of the Prince of Prussia. A monument to him is still in existence at the chapel of Serrières.

which she had heard: *Notre pauvre Suisse est dans un triste état. Imagine-toi qu'il y a au Locle un corps de vétérans de soixante-dix ans; ils tirent encore bien et peuvent empêcher le pillage. Mais tout le monde en voyant leurs cheveux blancs fondait en larmes. Accomplis ton devoir; tâche de te faire affectionner par les braves de ta compagnie; soigne ta carcasse!*

Mme de Sandol-Roy's letters to her friend Jeanrenaud sometimes refer to her friendly relations with Field-Marshal the Duke of York, Frederick, second son of George III, commander-in-chief of the British army and husband of the Princess of Prussia.

The year 1816 saw Jeanrenaud, the pioneer, as hard pressed as ever, working with renewed zeal and energy in this city where, far from his native land, he had succeeded in creating an atmosphere alive with friendliness, mutual assistance and cooperation. His young wife presented him with a daughter, Julie, to keep their eldest child company. But after a stay at Eltvil on the Rhine at one of the Souchay properties and a few weeks spent in Switzerland, he had a serious relapse. He was so racked by convulsive fits of coughing one day that he was unable to take the service. 'I have five or six critical years before me', he wrote sadly. But he was not to live through them ...

In the following year, as his health was deteriorating rapidly, he complied with his doctor's orders and left for Montpellier. People he consulted in Lyons advised him to remain there: 'I have dismissed my household, entrusted our little Julie to the care of my mother-in-law, and decided to move, with my wife, Charles and Miss Bury, the governess, to a milder climate.' When he had settled in the house of M. Caussanel, on the outskirts of a suburb on the banks of the Saône, he discovered that he was living a short distance from the quarters of Bleuler's Swiss regiment. It was a great comfort for him to meet Auguste Touchon again in Lyons; the latter was one of the best Neuchâtelois preachers, and pastor of the Reformed Church, his fellow-candidate for consecration, whom he had not seen for eight years and who, in spite of a whole suburb of mud and puddles to be traversed, was willing to devote all his evenings to him. What illusions this poor exile cherished: 'My health is quite good now and I think that I am at last on the road to recovery.'

From Lyons he wrote to his dear friend Mme de San-dol-Roy, first inveighing against the Genevan theologians whose disputes were a source of great glee to his Catholic neighbours, and then announcing the birth of a daughter and begging Mme de Sandol-Roy to be godmother to the child, jointly with his aunt, 'the two persons to whom I am most deeply attached in the world'.

This daughter was the future Cécile Mendelssohn Bartholdy. The following entry in the christening-register confirms the certificate of birth: 'This day, eighteenth of November 1817, was baptised by me, Cécile-

Jacques-Fs Petitpierre, the younger, 1774-1819.
Godfather of Cécile Mendelssohn Bartholdy.
Pencil-drawing by Abraham Girardet.

Sophie-Charlotte Jeanrenaud, daughter of François-Auguste Jeanrenaud, minister of the Reformed Church in Frankfurt, residing at Serein in the parish of La Croix-Rousse, and of Elisabeth-Wilhelmine Souchay, his wife. The child was born on the 10th day of October 1817 and was presented for Holy Baptism by her father and mother who named as sponsors Jacques-François Petitpierre, minister at Serrières in the principality of Neuchâtel, Charlotte Petitpierre née Droz, wife of the godfather, and Sophie de Sandol-Roy, née Barwell.' There follows the signature of Touchon as officiating minister. Following the usual custom, the child was given the names of her sponsors.

Shortly after, Jeanrenaud wrote to Mme de Sandol-Roy: 'Your godchild was christened three weeks ago. She is thriving and becoming quite a pretty little girl; doubtless her godmother has brought her luck. Moreover, she hardly cries at all. I hope she will keep to this line of conduct and that she will not justify the fears which her birth in this land of coquetry and malice inspire in you.' The allusion he makes to the beauty of Mme de Sandol-Roy was by no means exaggerated, for she was known in Neuchâtel as 'la Belle Anglaise'. Her marriage to Sandol had created quite a sensation: Sophie Barwell of Chertsey, born

Charlotte Petitpierre, née *Droz.*
Godmother of Cécile Mendelssohn Bartholdy.

near Portsmouth in the castle of Stanstead, travelled to France during the Revolution. Black-listed, in common with other suspects, she was imprisoned in the Abbaye, where she remembered François de Sandol-Roy, who had formerly been in love with her, but whose proposal she had rejected. 'Come and fetch your wife', she wrote to him. Thanks to his friendship with Barras he was able to obtain her release and was duly rewarded! A portrait of her by Reynolds which is now in Philadelphia is reproduced in this work and one cannot fail to be impressed by

Madame François de Sandol-Roy,
née *Sophie Barwell.*

Second godmother of Cécile Mendelssohn Bartholdy.
Painted by Reynolds. Private collection. Philadelphia.

the queenlike bearing of 'la Belle Anglaise', in her white dress and black plumed hat, her hair in curls and her hands tucked inside a muff. She has an expression of shrewdness which is revealed also in her letters. Jeanrenaud, in his misty retreat between the Saône and the Rhône, was kept *au courant* of all the gossip of Neuchâtel: there was a rumour that Monsieur de X, who had already had ten children by his wife, had now had another by the wife of M. de Y, the mayor, whom everyone knew was impotent. Jeanrenaud's comment was: 'This must have been the only noteworthy event in Neuchâtel since the visit of the King of Prussia!'

Jeanrenaud's accounts book, recently discovered, throws some light on his activities abroad between November 1816 and May 1818. In the midst of everyday payments for boatmen, medallions, theatre tickets, flowers, harpsichord tuner's fees or toys for Charles, one finds items connected with little Cécile-Sophie-Charlotte's christening: pastries, carriage hire, and a gratuity for the churchwarden.

During this period Jeanrenaud made a few trips to the Mediterranean and broke his journey at Nîmes and Montpellier; later on he spent some time with his friend Imer, the painter, who lived at Avignon.

But then, thinking himself quite well again, he returned to Frankfurt, where his place had been taken during his absence by Louis Manuel, later preacher at Lausanne, who published a collection of very fine sermons. Amid great rejoicing the divided household was reunited once more and again took possession of the cheerful rooms above the church, which were entered by a broad flight of stairs on the outer side of the wall behind the pulpit. The beautiful and spacious marble sanctuary, light flooding down from its lofty windows, echoed again the cheery tones of Jeanrenaud's voice as he stood facing the organ-gallery with its handsome colonnade, where all his parishioners were crowding to welcome him back.

The foundations of this church, resting on subterranean stone vaults supported by enormous pillars and fortress-like walls, were most unusual. The sanctuary itself, with the presbytery, the courtyard and a second building containing the parish hall, the consistory-chamber and the porter's lodge, made up a little world, an island of Calvinism in the very heart of the Lutheran country [1].

In June 1818 Auguste Touchon, who had been nominated minister in Hanau, moved closer to his old friend. Shortly before this time he had married in Lyons; later a famous sermon of his commemorating the anniversary of the death of Louis XVI was published. At this time Jeanrenaud, accompanied by his wife and Charles, stayed for a short time in La Chaux-de-Fonds in order to help his father set his business to rights. The clouds were finally dispelled in spite of the rascally behaviour of a certain

Front of the French Reformed Church in Frankfurt.

Above the oratory the apartments of Pastor Jeanrenaud are still to be seen (now 7, Goethe Platz).

---

[1] These buildings are still in good repair. To-day the pastor lives elsewhere and the apartments have been let to a layman, M. Johannes Kahler, but one can still see the lofty Louis XVI panelling in delicate grey, the piers with their sculptured garlands, the trophies, and the lovely rose-windows, above the marble-topped chests harmonising with the woodwork. A crystal chandelier, forgotten in the great salon which once saw so many faces, beckons to the beribboned

Postmaster Jeanrenaud-Racle, who was a stony-hearted money-lender and 'a scoundrel who calls himself my affectionate cousin although—thank God!—there is nothing we have in common save an unfortunate similarity of name!' Regretfully, Jeanrenaud had to decline an invitation from the Sandol-Roys, who were expecting a visit from him in their lovely country house in the Val-de-Travers. Time was short and duty came first.

Before another year had passed, Jeanrenaud's health had collapsed under the strain of overwork, and Touchon deputised for him on Christmas Day. Soon contradictory diagnoses and treatments for consumption hastened him to his death.

Pastor Touchon wrote touchingly of his friend's last moments to Mme de Sandol-Roy, telling her that he had died on the 16th April 1819 in the Frankfurt presbytery which was so dear to him. Jeanrenaud had fought an heroic battle against ill-health and on his death-bed he declared his simple, upright faith: 'Several times on the last day he prayed devoutly, but too inaudibly for one to be sure whether he knew his final hour had come. Sometimes he was able to recognise his wife and those who came into his room; and in his lucid moments he signed to them to embrace him. Here it is not the custom to accompany the dead to their last resting-place, but all the Swiss present in Frankfurt for the trade fair flocked to the funeral procession as if they had been at home. He always liked this custom and his family are glad that it was possible to observe it in his own case. His body lay in state for two days, the face uncovered, in his church, and he was surrounded by spring flowers; his features had not changed and were as fine as ever, and every one of his parishioners and others who came to pray at his side say how moved they were at the sight. He was buried nine years after

---

flower-baskets, and to the cupids dancing around. Jeanrenaud's library, his study where he wrote to his uncle the Dean or to his friend Mme de Sandol, and the many living rooms, previously invaded by the military, all are there. Nothing has changed. The church and the buildings belonging to it have the same purpose as before; sermons are still preached there in French, though less frequently now.

his arrival here, to the very day.' Certainly the death of this vigorous pioneer of the Protestant faith, this enemy of pedantry and useless polemics, was mourned as a most grievous loss by the whole parish, who remembered how many a time his inspiring example and unflinching zeal had infused them with a new vitality.

Louis Manuel (later the friend of Vinet) and Paul Appia, a Genevan pastor who came from Piedmont and who had been a rival of Jeanrenaud for the Frankfurt living and was subsequently appointed to it, delivered funeral orations praising worthily the great character of this fellow-Protestant. Thirty years later, in 1848, Appia, still minister in Frankfurt, was delving back into his memories and wrote thus to a member of the Mendelssohn family: 'Wishing one day to dream alone for a while, I went down to the old cemetery and sat on a bench near the wall, almost facing the entrance. Not far from me there stood a cross which I had seen many a time before; but on this occasion I had sought it out deliberately, for it awakened in my mind most vividly many old and cherished memories. Yellowed autumn leaves fell from the trees and swirled past me like fleeting symbols of human existence, and my mind went back to that day, forty years ago, when first I met the man who lies buried there. I remembered the light in Jeanrenaud's fine eyes and his sensitive smile, not without a touch of irony, which never banished entirely the natural gravity of his expression. His whole personality was filled with dignity and intelligence. As I recalled his shrewd appraisal of political or religious controversies I regretted deeply that I could no longer ask him his views and stimulate my own intellect by contact with his. Sometimes I wonder if moral qualities can be inherited... It is an obscure question, of course. But when I see his children and grand-children to day I would like to think it is so. May God grant my prayer that piety may bind together the lives and fates of all his descendants!'

So it was that the noble figure of Pastor Auguste Jeanrenaud passed away one morning in the spring of 1819. He left behind him a heart-broken wife of twenty-two and three babies, Charles, Julie and Cécile, and his wife had also to undergo the added strain of giving birth to a girl, Augustine, shortly after her husband's death. This child did not have even the joy of seeing her father's glance upon her, though he had gazed often into the wide blue eyes of Cécile.

Yet how can one remember a father whom one lost at the age of two years?

Cécile Jeanrenaud at the age of ten.
Silhouette in the possession of Mme M. de Coulon-Jeanrenaud, Miltenberg Château.

IV

YOUTH

The children of Pastor Jeanrenaud were brought up by their mother, more than a century ago, in the region bordering the Red and White Main, which flows from Bavaria, carrying along the sluggish waters of the Itz and the Regnitz from Franconia, the Tauber and the Nidda—the majestic Main which Charlemagne planned to unite with the Danube. In this district, then, the Jeanrenaud children lived, except for visits to Neuchâtel, and it seems that the pure, dancing, tumbling water might have the power of transmitting to a child who gazed on it each day, that transparency and candour of heart and soul which are the rare attributes of a few privileged beings, and which might not flourish so easily in a more immobile landscape. As yet the hand of man had not contrived, by building a system of locks, to curb the free flow of waters through Frankfurt, the ancient capital of that second Roman Empire extending from Schleswig to Palermo. Often, behind the severe windows of her mother's house by the river, Cécile Jeanrenaud, as a little girl, would stand on tiptoe and peer down at the lighters and cargo-vessels, and, mischievous or solemn, she would find amusement in the hullaballoo raised on the quayside by the screech of lifting-jacks, the rumble of casks rolling over the pavement, shrill whistle-blasts and husky shouts from stevedores, ferrymen and boat-towers. Her lingering gaze would follow the fluted trail of smoke rising from the river to form fantastic shapes, blurring the countryside with a hazy screen. Her vivacious little face, hair drawn back and fastened in a beribboned net, made a charming silhouette as she leaned from the bay-window of the tall and imposing edifice in the Louis XVI style, crowned by a gable with an oval-shaped bull's eye and bars, which was formerly the home of the Souchays and now the dwelling of the Jeanrenauds.

Carl-Cornelius Souchay had transformed the primitive abode belonging to his maternal grandfather, Baumhauer, into an elegant mansion. Next door to this palatial residence was another house which had also been restored, and which was called *Zum roten Mänche;* this had for many years been the property of his partner, the financier, Jean-Jacques Perret. These symmetrical structures, with their even rows of windows (barred on the ground floor) had no doors facing the river and so seemed, as it were, to shun the common herd and to be seeking refuge in aristocratic aloofness. The way out of the Souchays' house (built around a centre-court) was at the back and led into Old Mainz Street, where it is now known as No. 3. Crossing the threshold into the street, one walked right into the heart of the teeming city, which, even in those days, was overflowing *extra muros* and eating into the broad expanse of meadows. Gradually the motley new town spread itself in circles around its core of mediaeval buildings, huddled close together on either side of old country roads, like the hub and spokes of a wheel.

By the intimates of the family, the quayside residence where Cécile grew up was commonly referred to as the *Fahrthor,* though it must not be confused with the original Fahrthor, a gate-house with a long Gothic porch flanked by a tower with five spires, formerly part of the palace of the German kings, which stood near the wine-market. However, in order to distinguish this particular house from other town properties belonging to the Souchays, it was agreed to call it familiarly by this name, borrowed from that of the principal building in that quarter of the city.

For their daily walk, Cécile, her sister and their tutor, and indeed all the Frankfurters of the time, generally preferred to escape from the city by one of its fortified gates, long dark tunnels through which access was gained to the linden groves

The Fahrthor district of Frankfurt about 1830.

On the left are seen two neighbouring and practically twin mansions: one of them, *Zum roten Münche*, with a watch-house in front, was formerly the Perret Bank; while the other, known as the *Fahrthor* and the property of the Souchays, is the house where Cécile Jeanrenaud grew up; there, too, Mendelssohn's wedding took place in 1837 and there his widow died in 1853. The Fahrthor is, in reality, the battlemented building which originally boasted a Gothic porch in the middle; on the side stands the 'Revenue Tower', partially concealing the palace of the former German kings.

In the background are seen the Dom and the old Main bridge.

Watercolour in the possession of Herr Theodore Souchay of Marburg.

around the moat, bordered with quickset hedges. Often they would talk of the past splendours of this ancient and colourful capital, gracefully girdled with green. One could see, across the dismantled fortifications, the dome of St. Bartholomew at the centre of the city and then the tower of the proud and ancient

The Bergstrasse in Frankfurt.
Sketch by Cécile Jeanrenaud when a girl.

Römer keeping watch over the countryside and gazing at the distant Taunus range. Or else the Frankfurters could glance at the quaint old bridge spanning the river and the close-built houses of Saxenhausen on the opposite bank with their unbroken line of rooftops.

At the time when Europe, sickened by the Napoleonic Wars, was seeking refuge in Romanticism, firmly-rooted religious traditions tended fortunately to restrict sentimental excesses bordering at times on the grotesque. Everyone realises the inestimable value of a mother's presence with her children, but her loving kindness and god-fearing example become infinitely more precious when the father is dead. Each evening, summer, autumn, winter and fragrant spring, for year after year, Cécile's mother would lean over her cot to hear her youthful prayer and join with her in quiet thought. A soul nurtured in such an atmosphere of spirituality could not do other than bear rich fruit. From early childhood Cécile learned of the ephemeral worth of worldly fame and knew that only a pure and simple heart could rise above the pettiness of this world. Loving her work and finding pleasure in the arts, fond of wholesome delights, Cécile was to grow up to be a charming, almost ethereal being, radiant with freshness and grace.

It was with deep emotion that Cécile Jeanrenaud, at the age of sixteen, renewed her christening vows in the French church so dear to her father and so full of memories of his noble personality. She afterwards received communion for the first time in the presence of her Frankfurt friends.

Cécile Jeanrenaud.
Drawing in the possession of M. Paul Léo, Osnabrück.

On the occasion of his birthday, Pastor Paul Appia was presented with a delightful picture in oils by his young parishioner. She wrote: 'I had to hurry to get it done in time. Oilpainting sometimes makes me lose patience; but fortunately my good old master is amply provided with the quality. And then, after I had worked very hard for two hours painting the very fine faces of an Italian woman and her child, my master inadver-

The old Petitpierre house at l'Evole, near Neuchâtel, where Cécile Jeanrenaud stayed on several occasions. Drawing signed Grisel.

tently brushed against my canvas with his sleeve as he was leaving. This I did not notice until he had gone. I was in despair.'

The Jeanrenauds spent some time in Genoa and Turin with their cousin from Haarlem, Louise Petitpierre-Le Chevalier de Rochefort, so that Mme Jeanrenaud might recover somewhat

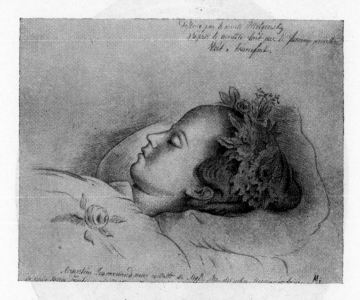

Augustine Jeanrenaud
Younger sister of Cécile, born after her father's death. Died at an early age.
Drawing by Count Miaczinsky.

from the sorrow caused her by the death of her little daughter Augustine, always a delicate child. Mme Jeanrenaud, who did all she could to keep alive their father's memory in the hearts of her three remaining children, often took them on a pilgrimage to the pleasant Neuchâtelois country which always remained their true motherland. There they spent many happy days with Charlotte Petitpierre, Cécile's godmother, whose house was perched on a rock at l'Evole, facing the lake, and in La Chaux-de-Fonds the Würfleins and the Pierre Jeanrenaud-Calames, recently married, greeted their relations with open arms. The three ladies travelled all over Switzerland to visit their numerous friends[1], making the journey in a private berlin-coach, the driver and horses being changed, as was the custom, at the posting-

Louise Petitpierre, née Le Chevalier de Rochefort.
Miniature by Convert.

---

[1] In Switzerland, and particularly in the neighbourhood of Neuchâtel, the Jeanrenauds had innumerable relations, with whom they kept in touch by correspondence as well as by visits. They also counted among their best friends the Du Pasquiers, the Bovets de Boudry, the Du Bois du Locle, the Combes, the de Bedaulx, the Monverts, the Grisels, the Berthouds, the Perrets, the de Bellefontaines, the Lardys, the Brandts, the Pahuds, the Coulons, the de Sandol-Roys and the Lorys.

The Lake of Geneva and the Alps, painted by Cécile Jeanrenaud.
Canvas in the possession of the Wach family of Wilderswil.

houses. Cécile spent some considerable time in painting, among other subjects, the scenery of Lake Geneva.

While the rain teemed down, marring the early part of July 1834, Cécile wrote from Berne, telling her friends how sorry she was to have left Neuchâtel, whose lake and mountains she still strained her eyes to perceive in the distance from the misty hilltops. Soon afterwards, the tall berlin, with the luggage stowed away on top under tarpaulins, was rolling on again, to the accompaniment of a cracking whip, towards Basle and Karlsruhe, on its way to Heidelberg where Cécile's brother Charles was studying law. The Jeanrenauds settled for their stay on the outskirts where 'the surrounding district and a long avenue of trees extending towards the plain recall the Allées de Colombier and the mountains of Yverdon; but alas!—the lake, which makes Neuchâtel so agreeable, is missing here, so that the comparison is imperfect.' From afar, amid the russet tones of autumn, they thought of the grapes ripening on the Jura slopes, and which 'Cécile would take such delight in arranging and tasting'.

Tékla Souchay, née Schunck, 1809—1876.
Cécile Jeanrenaud's aunt.
Photograph of a painting in oils, loaned by
Mr. John Edward Darnton, London.

The epistles addressed to Neuchâtel from now on were brimful of spontaneous gaiety, despite the loss through ship-wreck in the English Channel of five caskets full of precious possessions belonging to C. C. Souchay, all now lying safe in Davy Jones' locker. At Christmas time the cakes were adorned with a motif showing a pack of bears from Berne, fleeing from the dismal haunts of their capital, to seek refuge in 'Frankfurt, the hub of Europe', and show the Frankfurters their red sugar tongues.

Jean Souchay, merchant, 1797—1871.
Cécile Jeanrenaud's uncle.
Photograph of a miniature, loaned by
Mr. John Edward Darnton, London.

When Lory the Younger, the well-known artist from the banks of the Aar, came to the Fahrthor to show his fascinating Swiss landscapes to Cécile Jeanrenaud, she herself was already handling the brush with such sureness of hand, and delicacy of feeling and touch, that everyone was amazed at the quality of her work.

Fully absorbed in artistic pursuits and the cultivation of her very charming voice, Cécile gave but little heed to dances and other social functions. In a letter addressed to her aunt Charlotte in Neuchâtel and entrusted to M. Coulon, she wrote: 'We have spent a most agreeable winter. I say this not on account of the balls given by fashionable society in Frankfurt, which, to tell the truth, didn't amuse me vastly, but because we had staying with us my uncle Jean Souchay and his wife, of whom I am exceedingly fond. They have now gone back to England, where Grandpapa is to go himself this summer. Charles is here with us for the Easter vacation. He is sitting near me this very moment and smothering me in a cloud of smoke; in his blue palmleaf patterned dressing-gown he looks like a Turk puffing at one of those long pipes! I am so glad for you that winter is now over. You will be able to go into the gardens again, if not at six o'clock in the morning like last summer, at any rate for pleasant walks when the weather is fine. Here the trees are already showing tiny delicate green leaves.'

Cécile wrote to her cousin Cornélie Schunck too: 'When M. von Vrints invited me to another ball, I assured him that these aristocratic functions only bored me. My sister Julie came home quite early, although she enjoyed herself very much. She and Sophie Gogel told me all about it. I won a marvellous writing-desk in the guilds' lottery, for which M. Perrot had given me a ticket. I wish you could see the wonderful decorations inside and all the little drawers and hidden cubby-holes.' Such were the wholesome delights of a young girl who, although so retiring herself, nevertheless listened willingly to all her friends as they came in turn to tell her of their successes at the brilliant and fashionable receptions of the time.

Open house was always kept at the Fahrthor, where Fräulein Fischbach, the housekeeper, presided, but Cécile spent hours on end reading alone in the top-floor study, where the ceiling shimmered with the shadows reflected by the waters of the Main, dancing in the sunlight, and which had been a room much beloved by Cécile's mother as a child. Sometimes, when the house was filled to overflowing with relatives and friends, this panelled room was used to accommodate them.

Writing on the 2nd May to Cornélie Schunck, Cécile, known to be a lover of good music, happened to mention a well-known composer who, though unknown to her personally, was a friend of Fritz Schlemmer, a relative of the Souchays. Three weeks later this composer was to conduct the first performance of his oratorio *Saint Paul* in Düsseldorf. 'We had a letter from Fritz Schlemmer the other day, announcing the visit of M. Mendelssohn. I am delighted. But his charm has been so highly praised that I rather fear I may be disappointed in him. Tell Fritz I shall write to him later and let him know what I think of his friend... or rather, don't tell him anything.'

Though Cécile did attend dances and other social events occasionally, she seemed to be uninterested in prolonged banquets and ceremonies: 'I have to undergo a fearful torture: we shall have to spend half-a-day at table at the wedding of L. J. and F. de N., madly in love with one another, though neither of them is very prepossessing! And the children will make a dreadful row. You know how fond I am of pretty children, but I cannot stand noise.' But Cécile was not at all a kill-joy like the Huguenots who still could not forget the Revocation of the Edict of Nantes, after a century-and-a-half: 'At the theatre the other day, M. Clause amused me at least as much as the comedy itself!'

In truth, without her desiring it, this nineteen-year-old girl stood out from among the other girls of Frankfurt's aristocratic society. It is less her own, comparatively few, letters written during her youth, than the letters and diaries of her relatives and friends, which are most revealing concerning her true character. Her deep piety; her reverence for the memory of her father, of whom her elders had told her so much; a great love of the classics, combined with a romantic disposition—for romanticism was finding expression at that time in the most simple acts of everyday life—all these characteristics imbued her simplicity with an unconscious superiority, and enabled her to remain poised between two extremes: the Rationalism of the eighteenth century and the lyric sentimentality of her own age. Customs,

Cécile Jeanrenaud at the age of sixteen.
Pencil drawing in the possession of the Wach family of Wilderswil.

environment and circumstances were later to upset this balance and accord the victory to her heart, which later ruled her mind.

Cécile's beauty completes and enhances her portrait, and this was described by her mother in a few lines which were confirmed by the vivid testimonies of painters and writers: 'When we admire a pastel, do we not fear to spoil its delicate shading by removing the glass which protects it?' Thus, the most gifted pen could describe only imperfectly the charm and peerless beauty of which Cécile was possessed. From her earliest years, her whole being had something of the mysterious. At sixteen her exquisite figure and her carriage drew every gaze. Her dark blue eyes, shaded by long lashes and crowned by velvet eyebrows, shone with a radiant gentleness. It was impossible to see a more wonderful head of brown hair, a fresher complexion, or a more perfectly oval face. And to all her charms were added a delightful simplicity and naturalness of manner. The flexible quality of her voice soon permitted her to speak fluently in three languages. She was a good singer, but, much to her regret, somewhat delicate health prevented her from pursuing her singing studies as she would have wished. Drawing and painting were her greatest pleasures. Cécile was in no way egoistical; by her actions and by the sacrifices she was always so eager to make, she proved her affection and fidelity to those she loved. She judged herself with severity, but showed the greatest tolerance where others were concerned. She never raised her voice to scold and spoke but little, though her words were full of discernment. I still remember a remark made by one distinguished person: 'She likes to remain silent, but her silence is always eloquent.'

Many biographers have paid tribute to Cécile's exquisite beauty, some calling her a brunette, others describing her as blonde—and, judging from the lock of her hair which has been kept and which is amber-tinted, both descriptions were partly exact. She was a woman of rare character, combining uprightness and simplicity with extraordinary charm, and creating about her an atmosphere of fresh serenity. So much purity and restrained fervour breathed from her harmonious attributes, that her attractive personality was, as it were, veiled by a mist of distance.

For Cécile Jeanrenaud, with her unquenchable love for nature, seen through her artist's eyes, a pleasant countryside where birds sang was the high priest, the painter, the poet and the musician of God.

V

ART AND WORK

A tradition which has tended to become submerged by present tendencies, but one which should continue to honour old-established families, is the tradition of intelligence, of *work* and of *art*, for art is the universal religion of work, the very formula of the ideal which, thousands of years before the Christian era, was already implying the existence of God. It is this formula which shines from the golden lines of the Pythagoreans five centuries before Christ. It is perhaps possible that some sublime geniuses blossom forth from the bosom of their families like reeds in the desert, but others materialize after hard-won experience; they are complex and highly-developed souls which express themselves in many ways for the good or the pleasure of humanity.

The famous philosopher,
Moses Mendelssohn.
Silhouette by Lavater.

Felix Mendelssohn's grandfather, Moses Mendelssohn, the great German philosopher, a native of Dessau, was inspired by this noble, idealistic religion of work. I say *German*, because

Mendelssohn censured Frederick II severely for substituting French for German as the court language; also, his *Phaedo*, an adaptation of Plato's dialogue, became a classic; and his relations or intimacy with Herder, Kant, Winckelmann, d'Argens, Nicolai, Maupertuis, the Duke of Brunswick and Lessing emphasise the predominance of German, as opposed to other national inspiration, to say nothing of his translations of the Pentateuch, the Psalms and the Song of Songs.

In 1787 Mendelssohn the writer, his wife and their descendants were raised to the aristocracy. Before this the Marquis d'Argens commented on the application for this honour: 'A bad Catholic philosopher requests a bad Protestant philosopher to grant the privilege to a bad Jewish philosopher. There's too much philosophy in all this for right not to be on the side of the request.' Incidentally, a work of four-hundred pages has just been published in Amsterdam on the grandfather of the composer.

Among the descendants of this famous philosopher, Joseph Mendelssohn is worthy of note. He was an agreeable man, a scientist and a friend of Alexander de Humboldt, and his descendants are alive now. The first husband of Joseph's sister Dorothy was Simon Veit, father of the painter Philippe Veit; when she married again it was to Frederick von Schlegel, the publicist, Protestant historian and orientalist, known for his philosophy of history and his famous *Ancient and Modern Literature Course*. Afterwards in Rome and Frankfurt he held the post of adviser to the Ambassador at the Austrian Legation. Dorothy was converted to Protestantism herself, and her sister Henriette, who never married, became a Catholic. The latter became very friendly with the daughter of General Sébastiani, who was married to the heir of the Count of Choiseul-Praslin. Abraham Mendelssohn, a second son of the philosopher, lived at Hamburg until 1811; afterwards he settled in Berlin where he became a town councillor in 1819 and an influential banker, and where he was converted to Protestantism. This was the father of the composer.

On the suggestion of his brother-in-law, Bartholdy [1], later Prussian consul in Rome and owner of a famous villa there which housed many paintings of the German school, Mendelssohn the banker added to his own name that of Bartholdy (an estate on the Spree, a family property) and this served henceforward to distinguish his fine line of practising Christians from the other Mendelssohns. It was, then, in this remote period that the name of Bartholdy first appeared officially and it was to be perpetuated across five or six generations right up to the present day. It is to be noted that of the two lines descended from the banker Abraham Mendelssohn Bartholdy (from his son Paul and from his son Felix the composer) only that of Paul has a hyphen between Mendelssohn and Bartholdy. The

Abraham Mendelssohn Bartholdy, the banker.
Father of the composer,
Drawing by Hensel, in the possession of the Léo family.

composer's line then is the family Mendelssohn Bartholdy, without a hyphen, but as authors and biographers are generally unaware

---

[1] Jacob Salomon-Bartholdy, brother-in-law of Abraham Mendelssohn and uncle by marriage of the composer, was born on the 13th May 1779 in Berlin, of Jewish parents. He studied from 1796 and was converted to Protestantism in 1805. After taking part in the campaign against the French in 1809 as a lieutenant of the Viennese *Landwehr*, he joined the Prussian diplomatic corps in 1813 as Ambassador in Rome, under the name of Bartholdy. An enthusiastic lover of art, he brought the fresco into fashion again by inviting various German artists to decorate his luxurious home on the banks of the Tiber, which was called the Casa Zuccari or Bartholdy. He

of this distinction it is not wise to trust to their spelling in classing into one or the other branch the persons named or introduced in their works. Only a complicated genealogical table such as the one I have before me, showing all the descendants of the famous philosopher, allows one to see clearly the ramifications of a gigantic tree, still vigorous in spite of many intermarriages.

Now let us turn our attention to the personality of Felix Mendelssohn Bartholdy himself, his relations, his friends and his works before his marriage. It is interesting first of all to know what Emile Vuillermoz, the eminent Parisian critic, says of the composer. A few lines which appeared recently in the *Editions Cosmopolites*, convey better than any words of mine the impression that one should gain of him:

> 'Since contented nations and contented men have no history, one should on principle abandon the idea of writing a life of Mendelssohn, for indeed no one was ever more consistently and entirely happy than the composer of *A Midsummer Night's Dream*.
>
> 'His biography is like a novel by Zénaïde Fleuriot. The reader who has some knowledge of life and men wonders every minute if his credulity is not being imposed upon when such an unlikely character is introduced to him.
>
> 'One recalls the naive reaction of the Greek who urged the banishment of Aristides, explaining candidly that he was tired of hearing him called "The Just". When one considers the life of Mendelssohn, one reacts equally ungenerously. It is really wearisome to see Fortune heaping gifts on one of your fellow men with such openhanded perseverance and partiality. One feels confusedly that there has somehow been a miscarriage of justice. It is not thus that a human animal should accomplish his prescribed span in our vale of tears. Mendelssohn did not play the game.
>
> 'He was born into a family made up entirely of unusually intelligent persons, endowed with all the qualities and all the virtues. His father and grandfather were very remarkable men, exceptional creatures with wonderful brains and great hearts. He was surrounded by the most admirable lessons and examples.

---

died on the 27th July 1825, leaving two works: *The War of the Tyrolean peasants* (Berlin 1814) and *Sketches of the life of Hercule Consalvi* (Stuttgart, 1825). Various works of art and his collection of vases were afterwards transferred to the Berlin National Gallery.

This gentleman should not be confused with the French sculptor Frederick-Auguste Bartholdi, born in 1834 at Colmar. He took part in the Franco-Prussian War, and sculptured the *Lion of Belfort*, the *Vercingetorix* at the Musée de Clermont, the Lafayette monument and the *Statue of Liberty*, unveiled in 1886 in New York.

'One of the most profound and most sensitive influences over him was that exercised by Goethe. Mendelssohn made the acquaintance of the illustrious poet at Weimar when he was twelve years old. The proud old man took to the child immediately and insisted on keeping him in his company for quite long periods on several occasions. Little Felix was filled with respect and love while he enjoyed the society of the patriarch who was venerated by the whole of Germany. He never forgot the impression made on him by the great man. A new David, seated at the feet of Saul on his throne, he revealed to Goethe the mysterious realm of sounds and often assuaged the fevers of his genius.

'Mendelssohn's destiny gives the lie to all the so-called infallible axioms of the professional psychologists. The precocity of his talent did not render it ephemeral. He wrote an excellent symphony at the age of fourteen and at seventeen he put his name to that astonishing masterpiece, the Overture to *A Midsummer Night's Dream*. But his creative powers did not run dry and the magnificent output of his mature years did not suffer as a result.

'He was an amazing virtuoso and yet his music was not at all tainted with virtuosity. It was neither the music of a pianist nor of an organist. Neither was it the music of a conductor, although he had given proof of incomparable gifts as a choirmaster. He was a man who could tackle the most varied studies without dissipating his talents. He spoke several languages and read Greek and Latin fluently; he was also well versed in philosophy.

'Mendelssohn was handsome. Mendelssohn was rich, Mendelssohn was intelligent, sensitive, refined, elegant and endowed with all the advantages of home and family life.'

These few lines are extracts from a study which I would like to be able to quote in its entirety.

Felix grew up largely in the company of his delightful elder sister, Fanny, who was born in 1805 and who showed remarkable musical talent. He began learning to play the piano under the tuition of Mme Bigot—the interpreter of Mozart—and studied also under three masters of whom Berlin was justly proud, Frederick Zelter, Bernard Klein and Louis Berger. His brother Paul showed himself to be an excellent violinist and another of his sisters had a charming singing voice. All four children were baptised Protestants; they were well-behaved and astonishingly gifted and had the advantage of first-class tutors: Hegel, and Heyse, the celebrated philologist, among others; and they worked hard and enthusiastically to attain sublime heights in the art so dear to all Germans. Fanny was given to understand by her wise father that music could never be a career for her but must remain merely as an accomplishment: 'You must continue to see the matter in this light; because that is truly feminine and only that which is feminine befits a woman.' From then on she confined herself to helping Felix in his work: 'I watched his genius advancing step by step. I knew his opera by heart even before he had written a note of it.'

The child grew up, then, in an atmosphere of intelligent affection, free from those regrettably distant relationships which are so often a feature of family life in high society.

In 1821, young Felix was made to sit for a painter who was already famous but who later had an enormous success on the other side of the Rhine, Carl Begas[1]. Also during 1821, Felix jotted down in an album belong to his sister, Fanny, a sonatina which has remained unknown until now; it comprises eight pages, of which the first two are reproduced in this book.

His compositions were played first in Berlin in his father's house on the Promenade Neuve and then, after 1825, in a wealthy private house at 3, Leipzigerstrasse. At the age of eleven, having already composed a drawing-room opera, psalms, a double fugue, short symphonies, a quartet and a cantata, Felix made the acquaintance of Weber, who dined with his father one day just

---

[1] Carl Begas, a painter of portraits and historical scenes, was born in 1796 at Heimberg, near Aix-La-Chapelle, and was the son of a President of the Tribunal. From his earliest years he showed signs of great talent for drawing and painting. Encouraged by Phillipart, he worked in Cologne and then in Paris in the studio of Le Gros. When the Allies were in Paris the King of Prussia was struck by the perfection of a copy made by him of a Raphael Madonna and which the King saw in the Louvre. He bought Begas's *Queen of Heaven* and commissioned him to paint a picture with *Jesus on the Mount of Olives* as its subject. After this Begas worked in the cathedral at Berlin and while in Rome he completed his *Baptism of Christ* for the garrison church at Potsdam. He knew the Italian classics well and belonged to the same school as the other Düsseldorf painters. His portraits of von Schelling, von Humboldt, Ritter, Mendelssohn Bartholdy, Thorwaldsen, Rauch, Cornelius, Schadow, Leopold de Buch, Meyerbeer, Grimm, etc. are precious proofs of an extraordinary talent. From 1842 onwards he was attracted to Realism, as exemplified in his *genre* painting: *Three Girls beneath an oak tree* had quite a vogue. His work was popularised by innumerable reproductions. He became a member of the Berlin Academy of Fine Arts and died in 1854.

The composer's two sisters,
later Mmes Hensel and Dirichlet.
Drawing by W. Hensel, 1828.

after the presentation of his *Freischütz*, and filled the child with 'terrible respect'.

In the summer of 1822 Mendelssohn accompanied his parents on a trip to Switzerland, which began inauspiciously as he got left behind and forgotten at Potsdam, his parents noticing his absence between Berlin and Brandenburg. Naturally there was a great upset and all the carriages stopped; but his tutor eventually discovered him marching happily across the fields in an attempt to catch up with the rest of the party, armed with a cudgel and in the company of a young girl from thereabouts who was showing him his route. It was in the course of this trip across Switzerland that he made various pencil sketches of Neuchâtel and the Lake of Geneva.

Soon after this he met the Hillers for the first time, in Frankfurt. The young musician, Ferdinand Hiller, was to become one of his most faithful friends.

The following year, aged fourteen, Felix wrote, among others, a symphony which has been discovered quite recently and which Alfred Cortot played for the first time in Paris to an audience astounded by the skill, the unexpected maturity and the perfect knowledge of the classical art shown by this child. Moreover, his compositions followed fast on each other's heels and were later to fill about fifty volumes in the Berlin Library.

The large and noble old house in the Leipzigerstrasse was well suited to recitals of music. An immense *salon* was connected by a colonnade to another room, a sort of annexe for theatrical performances. Behind the house, which has since been converted into the Prussian House of Lords, there stretched a courtyard and gardens, lawns, a park, magnificent avenues of trees and a private forest, a peaceful retreat and a paradise for birds. Beneath a leafy dome there stretched a huge summer-house, the main body of which was an entrancing arbour which served as a sort of concert-hall. Over a period of twenty years, thanks to the co-operation of professional musicians, it was the scene each Sunday of concerts of an outstandingly high standard. Distinguished

Felix Mendelssohn Bartholdy.
Painted by C. Begas in 1821.
Replica by Horsfall, in the possession of Mrs. Albrecht Mendelssohn Bartholdy, Clifton Hampden.

foreigners, Berlin's high society, poets, artists, painters, sculptors, scientists, philosophers and well-known writers met in this *salon de musique* which was soon famous throughout all Germany. The *Garden Diary*, also called the *Tea and Snow Diary* offered the hospitality of its blank pages to the visitors, who covered them with serious or frivolous observations. Felix Mendelssohn Bartholdy was the life and soul of these gatherings which were followed by witty conversation and readings from Jean Paul and Shakespeare, among others. Klingemann's affection for Felix sprang from their meetings at these concerts which the Hanoverian diplomat, poet and artist attended on many occasions.

The following comment on these Mendelssohn Sundays was given by Camille Bellaigue: 'When one thinks of Felix in these gay surroundings amid this select public, heaped with—though not overwhelmed by—all the good things lent by this world and those given by God, marked out for genius and not called on to pay the price by any suffering, one ponders sadly (as he did, perhaps, himself) on other masters, even greater than he, but less happy: on Bach, buried in his refuge from the world, on Mozart, humiliated like a lackey, on Beethoven, a morose and solitary invalid. But what a welcome, in contrast, did life and fame give to Mendelssohn! How well received he was by both!'

1825 was the date of the Mendelssohn Bartholdy's move to the Leipzigerstrasse and also that of Felix' first visit to Paris, which he found disappointing. The music of Bach, Händel, Mozart and Haydn was almost unknown there, and petty rivalries divided the musical world of Kalkbrenner, Hummel, Rode, Rossini, Kreutzer, Meyerbeer and Cherubini. All these welcomed him kindly but he became friendly with only the elderly Cherubini, the great authority of that time, to whom even Beethoven deferred. Felix became annoyed when his sister and the rest of his family accused him of having a prejudice against Paris and attempted to justify and explain his attitude. Only truth, he said, had any real value for him, and if Paris was admirable in

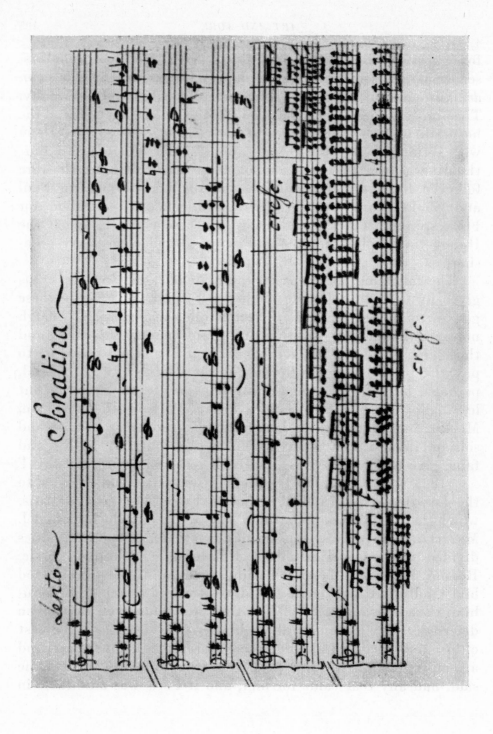

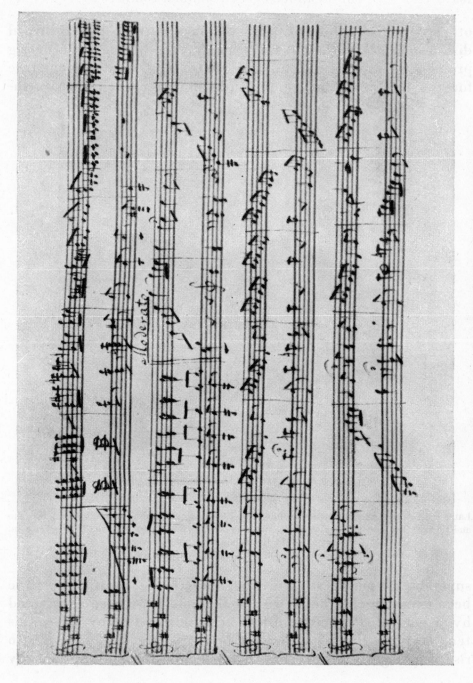

Opening bars of a sonatina composed in 1821 by Mendelssohn, aged twelve.
Unpublished, taken from an album belonging to his sister Fanny.

other respects it did not alter the fact that he had returned disillusioned. It was about this time that the Germans, becoming proud of their own great music, began to feel a certain repugnance for the less profound compositions of the French. Felix's in-

Old house belonging to the Mendelssohn Bartholdys,
Leipzigerstrasse 3, Berlin.

Later the Chamber of the Prussian Nobility. In 1900 a larger building was erected on this site and this also housed the Chamber of the Prussian Nobility from 1904 until the 1918 revolution. Later one of the Reich ministries took it over.
From a photograph taken in 1892, loaned by the City Library, Berlin.

superable aversion was surprising, nevertheless, for it might have been expected that his Jewish soul would have been captivated by a sort of Parisian musical eclecticism. In any case, this temporary disgust which he felt for Paris (the city was later to rise very high in his esteem), made of him the most specifically

German of all musicians. Indeed, it was he who brought Bach to the notice of the Germans who did not previously know his works, and Mendelssohn labelled the great music of Germany with a veritably exclusive nationalism. All great international music, he thought, should have a regional source.

The overture to *A Midsummer Night's Dream* was played first at Stettin, and there and elsewhere it aroused a frenzy of applause and enthusiasm among the audience. The rest of the score of this Shakespearian opera was not written, however, until fifteen years later.

In the spring of 1827 Felix began, at the University of Berlin, the completion of his education, for which he owed much to Hegel and Lichtenstein; his highly cultivated mind was a supplement to the almost disconcerting perfection of his unfailingly virile sensibility.

From an early age the boy had been obsessed by Johann Sebastian Bach's *St. Matthew Passion*, which, forgotten for a hundred years, had never been published. He managed to train a choral group to whom he taught this majestic masterpiece. Encouraged by Marx and Devrient, and in spite of the obstacles placed in his path by Spontini, he achieved his aim and, with the aid of the orchestra of the Academy of Singing in Berlin, the two first performances in March 1829 enjoyed an enormous triumph. This success resounded over the whole of Germany—at last a German musician had revealed to his land a predecessor who was to be the founder of a school.

Mendelssohn, however, always acted with complete disinterestedness, and never took advantage of his prestige and his authority as conductor to include his own works in the programmes out of their turn. Johann Sebastian Bach and Beethoven later owed a large part of their fame to him and the triumphant success of the recitals of the St. Matthew Passion caused Goethe to write: 'It is as if one heard the rushing torrents of the sea.' A boundless horizon was stretching before young Mendelssohn who was thus honouring his predecessor. In the words of Camille Bellaigue: 'He sealed with a golden ring, as it were, the marriage of his young talent to that of the elderly genius who was his compatriot, thus forging a fresh link in the chain of national tradition.'

Felix travelled first to England (not without discomfort on the crossing), to the land where Haydn, Händel, Mozart, Weber and Beethoven were so well loved, and it was English poetry with its particular delicate quality which inspired the *Fingal's Cave* Overture and the Scottish Symphony. He also wrote *Elijah* for the English, before whom it was first performed, and his letters give an almost naive account of the enormous success of his concerts in England. He was well received everywhere in the highest circles of the British aristocracy and left a trail of admiration behind him wherever he went. Felix had the great advantage in England of possessing all the accomplishments of an elegant man of the world: '15th May, 1829. Monday. Ball at the Duke of Devonshire's and display of oriental luxury. All Piccadilly was jammed with carriages; my cab was at the end of the line so I preferred to walk and wended my way towards the great stairway just ahead of Wellington and Peel, though I was not aware of this at the time. The scene was entrancing: brilliant illuminations, a whole series of princely halls, works of art everywhere, Titians, Correggios, da Vincis and the great Flemish masters. Lovely girls were dancing in this luxurious setting and dowagers weighed down by sparkling diamonds were seated on a circular dais. Enchanted and unrecognized I wandered among this elegant gathering. The whole palace is a marvel of good taste. An equally brilliant ball was given yesterday by the Marquis of Lansdowne.'

He mentions ten days afterwards a concert in the Argyll Rooms: 'I climbed on to the platform, brought my new baton out of my pocket and greeted the musicians; they repressed a smile at the sight of me, a mere boy, taking the place of their conductor with his powdered wig. The concert went off well and the audience were well satisfied and applauded furiously. The organizers came up to congratulate me and then there were introductions and handshakings. Clementi couldn't stop praising me. The evening will remain as one of my pleasantest memories. All these strangers became my friends in half-an-hour.'

Felix was, however, disappointed with a visit he made with Klingemann to see Walter Scott: 'We found Sir Walter Scott on the point of leaving Abbotsford and began by gaping at him like two half-wits. Fancy coming over a hundred miles and wasting a whole day for half-an-hour's trivial conversation. Altogether a rather bad business! We've taken rather a dislike to humanity's great men!'

A short time afterwards his carriage was involved in an accident in London and this forced him to give up the idea of going to Holland. He was also unable to be present at the marriage of his sister Fanny to the painter Wilhelm Hensel, whose albums Goethe asked to borrow, saying he wished to admire them at leisure. The recitals which Fanny Hensel held did much to aid the musical development of the Prussian capital. Another of Felix's sisters became the wife of Dirichlet, a greatly respected mathematician and scientist. Both Hensel and Dirichlet lived in the house in the Leipzigerstrasse.

The last meeting between Mendelssohn and Goethe—two of the few men whose lives were almost constantly happy—took place at Weimar before Felix's departure for Italy. He stayed for a fortnight with the greatest poet of his century who invited all the beautiful girls of the town to do him honour and who was loth to let him go:

'Each day before noon I have to play pieces by various great composers in chronological order, and explain to him how they contributed to the progress of the art, while he sits in a dark corner like Zeus the Thunderer; his eyes shoot forth lightning flashes. He was determined not to fall for Beethoven, but I played him the first movement of the Symphony in C Minor which nonplussed him completely. He began by saying: "That doesn't move me at all, it's just sensational and grandiose." Then he muttered a few more words and, after a long pause, he added:

"It's very great, absolutely amazing; it makes you think the house is going to fall down, doesn't it! Whatever would it be like if all men began to play that together".'

The author of *Werther* and the Baroness of Gustedt had the carriage which carried Felix away filled with sheaves of roses. He was bound for Rome, via Munich, Vienna, Venice and Florence. Goethe had given him a manuscript page of *Faust* with the following dedication: 'To my dear young friend, Felix Mendelssohn Bartholdy, the great and gentle master of the piano. In memory of delightful days in May 1830.'

Goethe often attracted painters as a subject. His best portrait, however, is that executed by the man who painted C. C. Souchay and his wife (the grandparents of Cécile Jeanrenaud) Carl Joseph Stieler [1].

Felix spent some time in Munich, possibly on account of two charming young girls, both of them fine musicians, Josephine Lang and Delphine de Schauroth; but after a disappointing stay in Vienna, where not a note was played of Beethoven, who had died recently, Mendelssohn found great delight in the Roman country. But at bottom his German soul jibbed: 'Get something performed here? It would be unthinkable. Italian music will always be like a Cicisbeo for me, vulgar and mediocre.' The only harmony he found in the Italian peninsula was the distant horizon, fading beyond the great stretches of the countryside. If the Italian Symphony—the first of his great symphonies—which he composed there, owes something to the visual enchantment he experienced, the work is, however, that of a Northern genius, the genius which was predominant in him.

---

[1] Carl Joseph Stieler was born at Mainz in 1781. He did only pastels and miniatures at first, but at the Fuger school, in Vienna, he took up oil-painting in 1815. He immediately acquired a reputation as a portrait painter in Hungary, Poland and in Rome and Paris, where he worked with Gérard. He painted an altar picture for the Leonhard Church in Frankfurt. In 1816 he went back to Vienna from Munich and painted a masterly portrait of the emperor. His portraits of Goethe, von Schelling, Tieck, von Humboldt, Beethoven and the royal family of Bavaria are also famous. His celebrated Gallery of Beauties in the Castle at Munich is also well-known. He died in this latter town in 1858.

Wolfgang von Goethe, 1749—1832.
Friend and admirer of the young Felix Mendelssohn Bartholdy.
Portrait by Stieler (photograph loaned by the State Museum, Munich).

Felix instinctively shied away from cosmopolitanism. He was a German and remained so, and thus as a musician also he was the most German of his *confrères*.

He attempted, moreover, with the help of Santini, to introduce the religious music of his own country to the Italians. Across the Italian border his friends were Vernet, Donizetti, Platten, and Thorwaldsen. In spite of a catholic spirit which enabled him to play melodies from *Cinderella* or the Overture to the *Barber* on the organ, he remained a fervent Protestant in the very depths of his being. Berlioz, who saw him each day, wrote: 'Mendelssohn is one of those artless souls whom one meets so rarely; he believes firmly in his Lutheran religion and I sometimes shocked him profoundly by laughing at the Bible.'

In the midst of the Italian landscapes on the banks of the Tiber, and even in the Sistine Chapel, Mendelssohn would have liked to be able to stop his ears so that music could come to him through his eyes alone! 'I have enough music in myself' he wrote, 'to wish ardently for a complete orchestra and choir again. Then, at any rate, one can hear what one calls sound; here there is nothing like that.' During this time he was obsessed by one of Goethe's poems which he worked tirelessly to transpose into his own medium. The result was the magnificent and lovely cantata for orchestra, solo and chorus, the *Walpurgisnacht*.

Next, Felix went up to Milan, where he divided his time between the Baronness d'Ertmann (to whom Beethoven dedicated his Sonata Op. 101) and Mozart, the son of the composer.

He tarried for some while in Switzerland and this time he had more leisure there. His two volumes of letters, published by his sons Paul and Carl in Leipzig in 1875 and 1882, contain much information about this 1831 stay in the country. In 1822 he had visited the Borromean Islands, had bathed in Lake Maggiore and saw Schaffhausen, Zurich, Altorf, Andermatt, Lucerne, Interlaken, Scheidegg, Meiringen, Geneva and its lake, where, in the Hotel Sécheron, he finished, at the age of thirteen, his Concerto in C Minor, which was printed as Opus 1 while he was travelling through Vaud, Neuchâtel, Bienne and Basle. In 1831, however, his various visits formed part of a solitary excursion which lasted for a year. Mendelssohn was now twenty-two. His first walk, armed with a haversack, was from Valais to Chamonix via the Col de Balme, and another walk took him to the Mer de Glace.

Every day he kept his diary, where he described the landscapes and mountains which met his gaze as he wandered up hill and down dale. When he composed music he showed himself to be a consummate master, and when he took up a pen he wrote as a writer. When he painted or sketched his albums of sketches and transparent water-colours were those of a professional.

A young girl called Pauline, charming in her Vaudois hat which she called a 'Flaschenhut', brought him refreshment and told him of the customs of her village. He described Italy to her and she introduced him to her cousin. He wrote home: 'I will complete my day by telling you that the Canton de Vaud is the most beautiful land I know, and the place where, when I am old, I should most like to live.'

Mendelssohn feasted on the wonders of nature which filled him with a new faith and transported him out of himself. He visited Boltigen, Wimmis, Weissenburg, and Spiez, where he composed *Hinterm Niesen, vorn am Niesen:* 'Just imagine glaciers and fields of snow, mountain peaks radiant and glorious in the strong sunlight. I think they must be a little like the ideas in the mind of God.' Terrific storms here and there formed a sharp contrast with the splendour of blue skies topping the mountain ridges. When a fair and a child crying in every key in turn prevented him from sleeping, and when the Simmenthal was as flattened as Brandenburg by the clouds, and chocolate-coloured torrents rushed in frenzied haste around the chalets, he went out walking, tirelessly, buttoning his jacket over his drawing book to protect it from the storm.

Switzerland was not, however, a source of musical inspiration to him, any more than Italy, except for a few minor exceptions. It is strange that he should be surprised that these untamed mountains inspired his old friend Goethe as little as they did himself.

Nevertheless, he visited Wyler, where he was brought a spoon when he asked for a boothook, and Unterseen where the bridges had collapsed (which produced three waltzes for posterity), he crossed the Grindelwald valley and climbed the Faulhorn and the Rigi, where he followed with difficulty 'a guide who ran along like a cat'; he also saw Hospenthal where some English people, drenched by a shower, were drying themselves before a stove, and Fluelen where the excessive patriotism of his compatriots was provoking them to advocate the annihilation of France. And then he bethought him suddenly of Schiller and at Engelberg he re-read his *Wilhelm Tell*. He was possibly unaware that the poet, reared on Rousseau, Shakespeare and others, was describing a Switzerland he had never seen.

The Engelberg monks who heard him play asked him to perform on the organ at the monastery on one of their feast-days. He accepted with joy and improvised. 'The head of the monastery stood before me, sang solos and conducted the choir of Benedictine monks with an enormous cudgel. I even had to play a march for them, very reluctantly on such an instrument. In the afternoon I played again for the monks alone. They gave me the most magnificent themes in the world, the *Credo*, among others. I improvised. It's the first improvisation I have ever wanted to note down and remember.'

A short time afterwards Mendelssohn was in Munich and in Paris. In Munich he gave several concerts at the Court and in elegant *salons* crowded with high society. His two agreeable girl friends became his pupils. Josephine Lang, 'one of the most adorable creatures I know, small, delicate and pale, with refined features and an interesting face—not beautiful—is so strangely striking that one can scarcely take one's eyes from her. She has a gift for composing melodies and singing them in a way which resembles nothing I have ever heard before.' As for Delphine

de Schauroth—who belonged to a family of barons of the Holy
Roman Empire—she was a remarkable pianist whom he was
delighted to see again. He dedicated one of his masterpieces to
her, his Concerto in G Minor for piano. A short time afterwards
Liszt surprised Felix agreeably at Erard's in Paris, by playing
it from the manuscript.

Mendelssohn was a plucky sportsman, an elegant dancer, an
excellent horseman, and was fêted by all spheres of society, but
he did not let his success go to his head. He made a rule of living
very simply. For instance, in Munich he received, quite inform-
ally in a shop which served him as a bedroom, innumerable
notabilities whose numbers overflowed into the road. Those who,
agog to hear him, could find no chair, settled themselves on
his bed!

Paris was his penultimate stop on his European travels.
There he saw Auber, Cherubini, Rossini, Paganini, Chopin,
Liszt, and Habeneck, the enterprising founder of the Conservatoire concerts. Baillot, the popular violinist, gave some recitals of chamber music in his honour. It was no longer the Paris
of six years previously! The opera and the theatrical works he
heard still displeased him, but he shared the ebullient enthusiasm
for great music with which the reawakened capital was vibrating:
it had just been shaken by the July Revolution. And then Mendelssohn's own compositions were played at the Conservatoire
and in church.

London was the last city he visited before his return from
his travels, so full of impressions and meditations. Here he was
accorded a veritable triumph. He played his Concerto in G Minor
and conducted *A Midsummer Night's Dream* and *Fingal's Cave*.

On his return to Berlin (a town of mourning now, for both
Goethe and Zelter were dead) the German essence of his personality had become concentrated and strengthened. In this there
was a great tribute to Germany. He rediscovered the pleasant
family life in the Leipzigerstrasse and saw once more the blue
undulating outlines of the Prussian plains, scattered with pine

Felix Mendelssohn Bartholdy.
Drawing by W. Hensel, in the possession of M. Paul Léo, Osnabrück.

Felix Mendelssohn Bartholdy, 1809-1847

Painted by Wilhelm von Schadow, at Düsseldorf, in 1835.
The property of Dr Felix Wach, Radebeul.

trees, and he exclaimed: 'My love for Germany is the clearest impression that I have after this long journey abroad.'

In a letter to Zelter, published at a later date, Mendelssohn had emphasised curiously diverse trends in the progress of great music. In Paris an initial centralisation of energies was to be observed, which was profiting a small local élite, but in Germany the opposite tendency was to be seen, for numerous regional centres had sprung up at the same time. It was true that Paris, where every talent was converging and which was enriching itself at the expense of the provinces, had a temporary advantage in results over the German towns where energies were dissipated; but it might well be that the lustre shed on the French capital by the Conservatoire, whose triumphs were unrivalled, would ultimately bring disaster. These tendencies were perhaps inherent in the different political regimes, but this was not at all certain. Certainly France's unity had just been reaffirmed. But when this was Germany's case also in 1871, it could hardly be said that Berlin was to overshadow other German towns by its own brilliance.

For this reason, when Mendelssohn was supplanted by Rungenhagen as successor to Zelter in the running of the *Singakademie* in Berlin, this was not as serious for him as it might have been. The Prussian capital was not at all the same to Germany as Paris was to France. In addition to the magnificent concerts which he gave in Berlin, Mendelssohn Bartholdy became the recipient of a particularly national honour. In April 1833 it was he—the youngest of all—who conducted the four hundred performers in the fifteenth Rhine Festival, the imposing homage rendered each year to the musical art by Düsseldorf, Aix-La-Chapelle and Cologne.

After the Düsseldorf festival, which gave him the opportunity of introducing Händel's *Israel in Egypt* to the public, he was appointed to the post of director general of music in this town. This was immediately after his return from London where he had often given magnificent concerts. It was perhaps his punctilious taste for music which was complete in itself and his

instinctive aversion to the theatre and opera (where modes of
expression are married so that one is the support of the other)
which made him wish to avoid the stage even as early as this
period in Düsseldorf. In this town particularly he popularised
serious religious music (discouraged by an inadequate orchestra),
but he later created a great masterpiece, the *St. Paul Oratorio*,
and it was played in Düsseldorf for the first time in May 1836.
It was here that he lived with the painter Wilhelm von Schadow [1]
who re-established the Academy of Fine Arts in the town and
did some very fine portraits of Mendelssohn. Felix—who conducted the new Rhine Festival at Cologne in 1835 (the year of his
father's death) was then offered the most sought-after post in
Germany, that of director of the famous Gewandhaus in Leipzig.

It was no small thing to have at one's disposal the only
orchestra in Germany which was absolutely accustomed to the
style of the classic masterpieces, to work in an atmosphere of
lively emulation between several choral societies, to enjoy the
advantages of being an unrivalled composer, an astounding
pianist (surpassed only by Liszt on occasions), an organist and a
conductor. Joachim said of him at a later date: 'As far as understanding and technical ability were concerned, Mendelssohn was
the greatest conductor I have seen. He exercised an indescribable
eletrifying influence over all his colleagues. He communicated his
spirit and his wishes to the orchestra and the singers by gestures
and signs which were scarcely perceptible, but supremely eloquent
and he was never guilty of exaggerated showiness.'

Leipzig, Bach's town and the capital of the realm of harmony,
the heart and brain of musical Germany, was anxious to attract

---

[1] Wilhelm Friedrich von Schadow-Godenhaus, son of a painter, was born in 1789. He
studied in Rome and met Cornelius, Veit and other German masters of the future there. For a
long time he preferred mystical and allegorical painting. He became a Catholic in 1814. His
frescoes for the Villa Bartholdy are: *Jacob clothed in the coat of Esau* and *Joseph in Prison*. In
1819 Berlin welcomed him as a professor in the Fine Arts Academy; he also decorated the
ceiling of the new theatre in this city. The garrison chapel in Potsdam is in possession of his
Adoration of the Magi. After 1826, Schadow presided over the Düsseldorf Fine Arts Academy.
His religious scenes adorn several German chapels.

the prince of conductors. After declining the offer of a professor-
ship at the University, Mendelssohn Bartholdy accepted modestly the highest appointment that could be offered at that time
to a musician. The destiny of Germany's favourite national art
had been given into his hands with the homage of his beloved
country. He was, then, thanks to the liberty with which he could
choose his programmes and to the magnetic splendour of the
lively capital of Saxony, the undisputed master of the music of
a whole region of Europe.

He opened his first concert in Leipzig with one of his joyful
resounding poems: *A calm sea and a prosperous voyage.* This could
be regarded as a symbol of the untroubled future in store for this
twenty-seven-year-old bachelor, with innumerable works already
to his credit, among them psalms, anthems, *lieder*, sonatas,
variations, preludes, character studies, fantasies, religious pieces,
dramatic compositions, vocal and instrumental music, bouquets
of wild flowers blossoming into blooms of a more exotic perfume,
symphonies, overtures, concertos and oratorios.

Mendelssohn had, however, only outlined his capacity; he
had not yet reached the zenith of his genius. He had certain of
his works which he wanted to complete, to allow to ripen or
to reshape, and others which were not yet conceived. Who was
to assist in this great maturing and facilitate his ascent to the
highest peaks of his art? Who was to share his exhilarating
existence and appreciate his temperament and the complex classic
expressions of a romanticist? Who was to become the intimate
and gentle confidante of this unwilling landscape-painter?

His father had said: 'I am afraid that in the end Felix won't
succeed in finding either a wife or a theme for an opera!' The
artist had, in fact, sought neither the one nor the other.

Geibel's 'Loreley' later served Felix as an opera theme
(though he composed only a finale for it). But let us pause to
consider the wife whom he chose, for the young girl who was to
make this great master even greater, was talented, charming,
and radiant with the joy of her first love.

Cécile Jeanrenaud, painted by Philippe Veit.
Oil-painting in the possession of the Wach family, Wilderswil.

VI

HARMONY

The most vital happenings are sometimes due to pure chance, and this is particularly true in the case of those people whom a conspiracy of events seems to destine for glory throughout their lives. In 1836, Herr Schelble, con-ductor of the Caecilienverein in Frankfurt, was ill and Mendelssohn, who took his place, stayed at his home. It was during this six-weeks stay in the town that he was introduced to the Souchays and the Jeanrenauds by his friend Fritz Schlemmer. It is worthy of note that, in order to rescue this Frankfurt choir, Mendelssohn gave up a trip to Switzerland and Genoa.

Senator Edouard Souchay
at the age of seventy.
(From a photograph).

Among other jottings in the diary of Senator Edouard Sou-chay, the brother of Mme Jean-renaud, is the following:

'When I went to see my re-lations one afternoon I met, quite unexpectedly, in the room they call "la salle", the director of the Städel Institute, the painter Philippe Veit[1], and a gentleman whom I did not know, but whom

---

[1] Philippe Veit, a German painter, born in Berlin in 1793, was grandson of Moses Mendels-sohn, the philosopher, on his mother's side. He spent his youth in Paris at the home of his father-

Veit introduced as his cousin, the conductor Felix Mendelssohn. Also present were my two charming young nieces, Julie and Cécile Jeanrenaud.

'I do not know why I was immediately conscious that this moment was a very fateful one. Herr Mendelssohn was pleasant and very distinguished. The look in Veit's dark, bright eyes seemed significant. Julie was gay, Cécile delightful but a little distant, as she always is. Her eyes were shining with deep enthusiasm.

'I heard my father's voice in the next room asking Herr Mendelssohn if he would be kind enough to play. It was only a short time since the death of his father and this seemed to be still affecting him—he seemed almost ill as a result. But, after first declining the invitation to play, he suddenly sat down at the piano as if he wished to express a mood—like Goethe with a poem.

> Was ich irrte, was ich strebte,
> Was ich litt und was ich lebte,
> Sind hier Blumen nur im Strauss.

'The following month my parents were away. Mendelssohn Bartholdy took advantage of the invitation to return and was a frequent visitor at the house of Mme Jeanrenaud, my sister, who

---

in-law, Frederick von Schlegel, and in 1808 he became the pupil of Matthai in Dresden. In 1811 he was in Vienna. After the war of independence, in which he took part, he went to Rome, where he worked, like Schadow and Cornelius, on the decoration of the Villa Bartholdy; he painted *Joseph and the Wife of Potiphar* and *The Seven Years of Plenty*. He also painted scenes from the Divine Comedy for the Villa Massimi, and the *Immaculate Conception* for the Church of the Trinita del Monti. His *Triumph of Religion* is in the Vatican. From 1831 onwards Veit directed the Städel Institute in Frankfurt. There is a great fresco of his: *The Adoption of Christianity and Art in Germany*, in this town and his frescoes *Italia* and *Germania* are well-known. It was he who immortalised the charming and ingenuous features of Cécile Jeanrenaud as a girl, and this hitherto unpublished portrait illustrates these pages; Veit also painted the portraits of Charles the Great, Otto the First, and Henry the Seventh in Frankfurt for the Römer. After 1843 he had a studio at Saxenhausen where he painted *The Ascension of Mary* and *The Two Marys before the Tomb of Christ* for the Frankfurt Cathedral. In 1853, the year of Cécile Mendelssohn Bartholdy's death, Veit, now living in Mainz, was drawing the plans for a series of religious subjects for the Cathedral. He died in Mainz in 1877.

lived on the second floor facing the Main. The composer made various sketches from the windows of the house.'

In July 1836 Cécile Jeanrenaud wrote from Frankfurt to her cousin Cornélie Schunck in Leipzig, whom Mendelssohn knew well; the latter undertook to deliver, in the course of his travels, messages written by the two girls to each other.

'I meant to write to you from Heidelberg where I have been staying with Aunt Benecke. My aunt and uncle were away, but the little rabble didn't make too much of a rebellion without their sovereigns; when there were arguments we had recourse to a higher authority. Julie and I supervised the piano lessons. You need a lot of patience to listen to those little fingers scampering about and see all those funny faces the youngsters pull when they are counting: "Hélène, don't screw up your mouth! What's that face for? Sit up straight." The child is making progress, though, because she's very eager to improve.

'Talking about the piano, I suppose that all of you are improving. I hear you play with Herr Mendelssohn. I would never have the courage for that, though he was very indulgent about our Caecilienverein chirpings! We talked very happily while he was sketching scenes from the window of the house.' One of Mendelssohn's sketches, done at the window of his future fiancée's house, is reproduced here.

It had never entered the head of Felix's mother that he might be in love or wish to marry. He was accustomed to the flattery of women and paid no attention to it, and he had never given grounds for any gossip. So that when, in August of that year, rumour had it that her adored son was extremely interested in a young girl of whom she did not know even the name, his mother was on the point of collapse. Mme Hensel wrote, in order to comfort her: 'Dear mother, I beseech you not to worry, at the age of sixty, because you think Felix is in love! Couldn't Dr. W. give you a sedative to calm such youthful feverishness? I share your emotions and the suspense is making me quite nervy. But we mustn't worry. Felix is a man of taste. I've got a vague suspicion. Is it perhaps a Miss Jeanrenaud or a Miss Souchay?'

For her part, Cécile Jeanrenaud, seeing Mendelssohn for the first time, had been amazed. In Frankfurt, during her childhood,

The Fahrthor and the Main at Frankfurt.
Drawing by Mendelssohn from a window of his fiancée's house.
Property of the Wach family, Wilderswil.

she had imagined this famous personage as a morose old man, inaccessible, with a satin cap, playing interminable fugues. Thus, the reality had engendered in her a modest feeling of attraction to the young man. She wrote to her cousin: 'He'll talk to you about us when he returns to Leipzig from this seaside stay which he says he is not looking forward to as he fears he will be bored. Mummy and I assured him that wouldn't be the case

Felix Mendelssohn Bartholdy.
Drawing by his brother-in-law, Wilhelm Hensel, in the possession of M. Paul Léo, Osnabrück.

at all. And then we made a little bet ... I shall be glad if I win...'

Mendelssohn came under the spell of Cécile Jeanrenaud from the start. He felt that she could be the ideal and exquisite wife for an artist. He confided every day in his close friend, the German poet and musician, Ferdinand Hiller, during their walks together. At this time Hiller did not yet know Cécile. During his ever more frequent visits to his beloved's home, Felix was so reserved that Cécile herself believed he was more attracted by her mother's brilliance, for the latter was vivacious, intelligent and cultured and talked the picturesque Frankfurt *patois* to perfection. It was only very gradually that the composer finally began to pay his attentions to the girl. Hiller claimed that Frankfurt society was following with undisguised curiosity this half-veiled courtship. He even added: 'Various remarks which I heard made me see that in certain circles it was considered scarcely sufficient to have had a good education, to be successful, pleasant and cultivated, to have achieved fame and even to belong to an illustrious family, in order to cast one's eyes in the direction of a young patrician girl of Frankfurt. But I don't think these comments ever reached Mendelssohn's ears.' The Hiller family were then living in a flat *Zum Roten Mänche*, the former dwelling of the Perrets, and the twin house with that of the Souchays. Mendelssohn Bartholdy often went from one to the other and informed his friend of the thrilling progress of his love-affair with much enthusiasm: 'The thing was so serious that it wasn't possible for him to begin by talking to me of anything but his love.'

Wishing to put his feelings to the test, Felix forced himself to leave Frankfurt to stay with his friend, the painter Wilhelm von Schadow at Scheveningen. This was the seaside holiday mentioned by Cécile. When one is in love there can be no victory but flight. On August 8th he wrote from the Hague a long letter to Hiller, of which a few scattered sentences follow:

'I think I shall turn into a cheesemonger here and never return. If you were in my place you would have packed your bags ten times over! Each morning at 8 o'clock we go to Scheveningen to bathe. The sky is always mysterious and inscrutable. Fish and shellfish stirred by the waves on the shore. Monotonous dunes. A Dutchman assured me that I should find majestic inspiration here. There are a lot of music lovers who get annoyed if one wants to say "Oh, to the devil with music!" Ladies from Leipzig parade on the promenade with their hair coming down in a fine dishevelled state—quite terrible! One ought to make love to them, I suppose, and then it might be better. Do you remember our long walks at night by the Main and my despairing confidences on your sofa. What is happening to the Caecilienverein? Doth it live, sleep, snore? Tell me all about Frankfurt. Tell Mlle Jeanrenaud that I've a print of Toulon here in my room and that I think she is a Toulonnaise. If you show this letter to a single soul, may you be hanged or roasted! Destroy it. Burn it. Reply by return.' A water-colour painted at that time shows the beach at Scheveningen, with a property belonging to the Wied family overlooking it.

Ten days later, alone, without Schadow who on his side had been unable to settle down, he announced his early return: 'I shall stop with my uncle at Horchheim and on the 28th August I shall celebrate Goethe's birthday with some Rhine wine!'

It is certain that absence, that adept at the creation of mirages, and lonely walks on a sun-splashed shore, are liable to conjure up an even more clear-cut picture of an entirely wonderful and utterly pure girl with whom one is in love. Would Felix be able to stem this mighty flood of new sentiments and win a victory in the struggle which, in spite of his jokes, was taking place in his heart? In what frame of mind did he set out again for Leipzig and Frankfurt? He was of age and he was famous throughout Europe, but he picked up his pen and wrote respectfully to his mother: 'I'm asking you to let me act as I see fit for my own happiness. Tell me that you trust me and that I am freely granted the liberty which I have already enjoyed for a long time. You know that I shall not abuse it. I will make up

View of Scheveningen about 1837.

Watercolour by A. Schelfhout (Municipal Museum, The Hague).
(Photograph loaned by Mme W. van Veen-Coenen).

my mind when I see this exquisite girl again. We still know each
other very slightly: I can't tell you much about it. I know that
her presence has afforded me some wonderful days at a time
when I was longing for them and when I needed them; I know
that she is the daughter of the late Pastor Jeanrenaud, that she
has been brought up by her mother with infinite tenderness and
care, that she is called Cécile and that I think she is very nice.'

Perfect harmony? Why should this artist, already possessed
of unbelievable good fortune and who, to crown it, was called
'Felix', why should he not add a string to his lute? Why should
he not marry 'St. Cecilia', patron saint of music?

Was not the defeat of this exceptional, talented being, of
this fresh, joyous and pure soul, in fact a victory? A mystic
force was drawing the sweetest and most lovely girl in the world
to him? What did Senator Souchay think of it?

'Herr Mendelssohn had great difficulty in leaving Frankfurt
each time he had to go. By mutual agreement an excursion to
Kronenthal in the Taunus was arranged, and it was there,
beneath the shade of the fine beech trees, that he declared his
love to my niece; his feeling for her was not without an answering
echo. My business prevented me from going on this excursion
but I greeted my new nephew with great joy that same evening.
Although it was fashionable to decry Frankfurt, Herr Mendelssohn, a much-travelled aesthete, had a vivid appreciation of the
charm of our town and the surrounding country.'

He went on: 'Cécile was slender and well made. Her eyes
were blue and her expression enthusiastic and mischievous. When
she spoke one noticed her delicate, pretty lips eager to talk,
and a strange fleeting invitation to chastity and love. She was
not, perhaps, exceptionally musical . . . she preferred her fiancé
to music . . . but she was a most perfect example of a serene
woman, always peaceful, gentle and helpful, and that is doubtless
what Herr Mendelssohn needed.

'My sister, Madame Jeanrenaud, loved him like a son from
the very day of the engagement—and like a son whose innermost

heart one has known from childhood. He was not at all one of those sons-in-law who have been selected and hand-picked from one's kith and kin, but he was sent by Providence straight from Heaven, where good marriages are made. My sister's friendly nature, and her spontaneous kindliness about her friends, attracted Herr Mendelssohn greatly. When he was able to spend long hours admiring the tranquilly-winding Main from the windows of his "Little Mother", as he called her, and feeling his dearly beloved Cécile close to him, then his happiness was inexpressible.'

Felix's own 'Tagebuch' confirmed this account. Each day he composed in the morning. He found pleasure in examining the manuscript scores of Mozart's *Don Juan* and *The Magic Flute*. In the afternoons he paid visits and went for walks. One day he called on the Jeanrenauds who were on the point of going out. But he was compensated for this disappointment the following Sunday, when he lunched alone with Cécile. He often saw Philippe Veit who painted a portrait in oils of his fiancée; he also saw Schlegel, Passavant and Chopin, whom he met at Hiller's house.

Cornélie Schunck, in the country at Prisnitz at that time, received a letter, signed by Cécile and Felix, and dated Frankfurt, 6th September 1836: 'You must forgive me for leaving your two letters without a reply. I have a very guilty conscience about it, cannot bear to think of your being sad, and must confess that music is not the only cause of everything. These last few days have been trememdously happy ones for me. I have just got engaged and I can well imagine your surprise. I can scarcely believe it myself. Every good wish and my love to you. You'll see that my news is confirmed by a name which you know well and which you will find here beside my own. Affectionately yours, Cécile Jeanrenaud. Felix Mendelssohn Bartholdy.'

On the 12th September they wrote, also together, to Charles Jeanrenaud—*poste restante* at Neuchâtel. Charles was Cécile's brother and seems to have been playing truant in the town: 'I don't know quite how to tell you what has just happened, little brother. I would much rather you were sitting quietly here with me, so that while I told you of these marvellous things I could stroke your curly hair. If you dropped off to sleep, as you do sometimes, and I said suddenly: "My dear little brother, I am engaged, I love another man besides you with all my heart!" then you would, I know, jump up and, red with anger, you would say: "Ungrateful wretch!" I would ask your forgiveness quite gently . . . on my knees, perhaps, and I would go on: "Why were you away so long, Mr Brother? Why did you bother so little about your small sister? You were so busy, so preoccupied. So why, then, should your nice sister not take advantage of her liberty to get up to some tricks? So go back to sleep while you grumble and call me your "Knörzerchen"!

'The secret of these lines is explained by a name which you see here, together with mine. Tell me that you adore me as always. Your loyal sister, Cécile.

'May I personally tell you of my immense happiness and, at the same time, of my sadness that you are not here. Grant me your friendship and your brotherly love. I would be so glad if your first impression was not that a stranger was going to intrude on your family. Anyway, such a feeling must not be uppermost in your heart before we have seen each other and talked together. My whole happiness depends on your sister—I don't deserve such happiness but I cannot live without it. Let us hope that we shall meet this year. Perhaps I shall be in Frankfurt when you return?

'With the hope that, for both our sakes, we shall be excellent friends, I am yours very sincerely, Felix Mendelssohn Bartholdy.'

Let us take a few extracts from other lively letters from Cécile, all hitherto unpublished. She did not know Leipzig and was very pleased to spend some time there with her relatives the Schunks. On the 19th September of this same year, 1836, she wrote: 'How strange it is to be engaged, my dear Cornélie! Unfortunately I shall have plenty of time to get used to it. It isn't official yet, but all the town is talking of it . . . however, it can't be helped! At first I felt a sort of secret shame. I contemplated myself in the mirror on my pretty desk. It seems that I have changed these last days—or is it the mirror? Aren't I being quite absurd! But everything is upside down in my heart.'

After the happy engagement had been announced at Neuchâtel, Mme Jeanrenaud sent an affectionate message to her son Charles on the 9th October:

'You are quite right, my dear, to be surprised at my long silence. But if you knew how our existence has been in a positive whirl these last weeks you would find it natural and forgivable. I think that when you know your future brother-in-law you will love him with all your heart and thoroughly approve Cécile's choice. At Christmas—God willing—we shall all be together. We'll talk about Neuchâtel then. Think about M. Bovet, of Boudry, and his son with whom I had a talk lately about the Mercier business. I have just thanked Mme Du Pasquier for the hospitality she showed you.'

On the same day Mme Jeanrenaud wrote to her aunt Charlotte Petitpierre:

'My brother and my sister-in-law left on Monday with the young Rothschilds. We spent a day with them and Mme Mendelssohn, Felix's aunt, who is a very tall and beautiful lady. She was going to Berlin. In the evening Count Léon de la Borde paid us a visit. To-morrow I expect M. Bendemann, one of the most distinguished young painters of Düsseldorf and very friendly with M. Mendelssohn. You see, my dear Aunt, that life is very gay with us. My love to Julie and Alphonse. I have written to Cousin Louise in Haarlem to announce Cécile's marriage myself and to tell her our news. Your affectionate niece, E. J.'

On the 10th October, her own birthday, Cécile wrote to Cornélie Schunck, her *confidante*: 'Thank you very much for all the kindness and affection you have shown to Felix, my dear. The presence of all your family in Leipzig is a wonderful balm which helps us to bear our separation. Why is Felix so depressed when he thinks he isn't going to get a letter? I am looking forward to coming. Fritz Schlemmer gave us a surprise by arriving very early in the morning. He tried to make us think it was Felix and had himself announced as a gentleman from Leipzig, but no-one was taken in! Just think! I am nineteen to-day. What a child I am still!'

When Cécile took up her pen in the middle of November, in very cold weather, it was to say: 'The winter is as disagreeable as M. Hanck; I am building castles in the air for next summer. Here life is terribly dissipated! Nothing but balls and yet more balls. It has been snowing for three days. Instead of going for walks we are sleighing. This morning there were fourteen sleighs on the Rossmarkt and a lot of gentleman driving them, who were all busy trying to catch the eye of the ladies as they drove...'

At Christmas the director of the Leipzig Gewandhaus came to spend three weeks in Frankfurt with his fiancée:

'Dear Mother, now I am back in my room I must announce to you my engagement to Cécile Jeanrenaud. My head is in a whirl with everything that has happened these last days. It is late and I don't know how to tell you, but I simply must write. How rich and happy I feel. Your letter is in front of me—I've opened it to make sure you are well, but I can't read it. Good-bye and think of me.'

On the 13th December it was Fanny Hensel's turn to get some news:

'Yes, my dear sister, here I am settled at Cécile's desk. I am wonderfully happy. How can I tell you of my joy? My only worry is the prospect of the 163 calls which we are to begin making to-morrow. What do you think of that? I am being shown no mercy and no-one will take any pity on me. What does it matter though! I am much too happy to make a fuss.'

A few days before Christmas Fanny thanked Cécile for a drawing which the latter had done herself, and took the opportunity of saying a word in praise of her husband, himself a painter: 'I can say the same of him as you do of Felix: "his talent is the least of his qualities". She continued: 'Dear friends, is it really right to have to pay 163 calls? But it's absurd! We've worked it out several times and it seems that if you deal with twenty a day you'll need all the week. But that's no way to live! It's quite barbaric! I hope that one of you will sprain an ankle after the third visit or catch a cold which will keep you in your room for the rest of Felix's stay in Frankfurt. The thought of having to make those 163 calls again after your marriage will possibly give you the idea of having the ceremony in Leipzig? What a pity you won't be here to-morrow. We are having a pretty celebration and are going to illuminate our two big orange trees in the hall; the Christmas trees will be set up in the blue room.'

After a merry Christmas at the Fahrthor, in a warm and intimate family atmosphere and amid surroundings filled with a pious Protestant spirit with which Mendelssohn Bartholdy felt himself very much in harmony, the date of a more significant ceremony—that of their marriage—was not far off. Before returning to Leipzig, he sent a few lines to his sister, Frau Dirichlet. These seem to be paradoxical when one thinks of the new inspiration which his love gave later to his talent: 'I am madly in love. It is the first time in my life. I have to leave Frankfurt to-morrow and I am filled with indescribable unhappiness on account of it. I owe the first really happy hours of this year to this too charming girl. What can I do? I can neither compose, nor write, nor settle down at the piano—I can scarcely draw. That's the state I am in!'

After Mendelssohn's departure for Leipzig, where he was required to conduct his oratorio *Saint Paul* on the 16th March, and while the news of his forthcoming marriage was being announced in papers and gazettes, his fiancée was complaining: 'I've been spoilt, why does this terrible thing—separation—exist? He is already far away and my mood has nothing of the rosy hue of my note-paper!'

For fear lest these two young people should pine away, one for the other, it was decided that the marriage should take place on the 28th March in Frankfurt.

In 1837 Frankfurt was the mercantile centre of Europe. It was there that the brilliant fairs, which stretched from the Fahrthor to the Old Bridge on the Römerberg and the banks of the Main, took place. In the spring and autumn long lines of carriages and carts were uncovered in fantastic bustle and

Frankfurt about 1840.
Oil-painting by Carl Morgenstern, presented by the Town Council to Senator Souchay.
Property of M. Théodore Souchay, Marburg.

excitement. Amid this hurly-burly, this collection of stalls, with jewellery, silk, velvet, trinkets, belts, buckles, toys and every imaginable article, all polished and shining—the crowd of sharp-eyed buyers made their way. Plantin Moretus sent thousands of books and prints which were absorbed by customers as readily as vapour by the sun. How many times must Cécile Jeanrenaud have been entertained by this amazing display of miscellaneous objects, side by side with lemon-trees in bloom, pomegranates, myrtles, narcissi from Constantinople, hyacinths from Brittany, asparagus tips from Germany and Lyons, honey from France, cherry brandy, bergamot caramels, nut sweets from Turin, nectarines from Provence and Pavia, figs from Calabria, spaghetti from Genoa and Sardinia! And what a strange sight it was when all this crowd of merchants pressed together into the inns and took it in turns to feed in the cook-houses. But the odour of local activities was to grow faint and the picture of the scenes grow dim in Cécile's mind, for she was soon to leave the banks of the Main. One can see the style of the old houses which ran along the quayside, in the canvas painted at that time by Carl Morgenstern[1].

Felix Mendelssohn's popularity was such that everyone wanted to be associated with his happiness. The people of Leipzig—in their fashion—wished to celebrate the engagement of this great musician, this great German patriot who did them so much honour. One day when the finale of *Fidelio: Wer ein holdes Weib errungen*, figured in the programme of a concert, the crowd grasped the allusion and obliged the artist, by shouts and frenzied applause, to improvise at length on the nuptial theme.

In Frankfurt on the 28th March, 1837, there was a most affecting ceremony, and one which was both distinguished and dignified.

Barouches with smartly-dressed coachmen, and coaches covered with flowers brought an elegant crowd of relations and friends across Frankfurt from the Fahrthor to the French church, along the old streets. The long lively procession left behind it the blue and emerald facades of the old city and the wrought iron gables standing out against the crystal sky.

Soon after the arrival of the procession before the church, chains were carried across the Allée beneath the trees to bar the

---

[1] Carl Morgenstern, a landscape painter, came from Dessau and was born in 1811. He was the pupil of his father, the excellent painter Jean-Frédéric Morgenstern. He was influenced first by Christian Morgenstern and Rottmann in Munich. After travelling in Italy, to Nice, in Holland and then in France again, he settled in Frankfurt. Many German museums and private collections have examples of his charming and luminous works. In particular one can see some remarkable landscapes of his in the Städelschen Kunstinstitut in Frankfurt: *Rheingrafenstein*, near Creutznach, *The Port of Pozzuoli*, near Naples, *The Grand Canal*, at Venice, and the portrait of Frau Elsa Langwort. Carl Morgenstern died in 1893.

Interior and pulpit of the French Reformed Church in Frankfurt.
In its former and present state, Goethe Platz.

way and enforce silence. At the foot of a Louis XVI pulpit, decorated with urns and supported by double marble columns, and opposite a wonderful show of greenery and sheaves of magnificent flowers, in a church packed even to the organ gallery where one of the composer's works was being played—Cécile and Felix stood modestly together, before kneeling at this solemn and romantic moment in the presence of God and his witnesses. They vowed to serve Him and promised to help each other loyally as long as they should live.

Pastor Paul Appia, with his benevolent expression and his patriarchal beard, preached a sermon on the very appropriate text taken from the Psalms, Verses 1 to 5 and 12 and 13 of Psalm XCII. In this Protestant and Calvinist sanctuary the Genevan pastor reminded his congregation of the great theologian Ostervald who was a compatriot of the Neuchâtelois bride and whose name was constantly on the lips of thousands of people in Germany:

> *It is a good thing to give thanks unto the Lord and to sing praises unto thy name, O most High:*
>
> *To shew forth thy loving kindness in the morning, and thy faithfulness every night,*
>
> *Upon an instrument of ten strings, and upon the psaltery; upon the harp with a solemn sound.*
>
> *For thou, Lord, hast made me glad through thy work; I will triumph in the works of thy hands.*
>
> *O Lord, how great are thy works! and thy thoughts are very deep.*
>
> *The righteous shall flourish like the palm tree: he shall grow like a cedar in Lebanon.*
>
> *Those that be planted in the house of the Lord shall flourish in the courts of our God.*

Let us now take some extracts worthy of quotation from the inspired sermon pronounced by M. Appia; I have a copy of this sermon before me, written in Cécile Mendelssohn Bartholdy's

hand for her cousin Alphonse Petitpierre, who was prevented
from being present at the ceremony:

> *'Your Christian marriage will be a hymn, an unceasing*
> *song in praise of the Lord. Believe this as you give each other*
> *your hands before the altar*
> *of the infinite mercy of God.*
>
> *'Show your gratitude to*
> *God for the many benefits*
> *of body and soul with which*
> *He has endowed your youth*
> *and which He now crowns*
> *in the fulfilment of your*
> *dearest wishes for this*
> *world. Lay these gifts before*
> *his throne and say together:*
> *these we consecrate to thy*
> *service. It would seem that*
> *your lives are destined to*
> *be untroubled by the ma-*
> *terial needs and interests*
> *which govern those of most*
> *men and women. What is*
> *most sublime in the Arts*
> *will, in any case, embellish*
> *your days together.*

Paul Appia,
Pastor in Frankfurt from 1819—1849, who
officiated at the French ceremony of the
Mendelssohn Bartholdy-Jeanrenaud marriage.
Pencil drawing belonging to the Appia family,
Paris.

> *'The angels who sang*
> *around the cradle of the*
> *world sang also over that of*
> *Jesus Christ and the ce-*
> *lestial army repeated in chorus: Glory be to God on high,*
> *peace on earth and good will to men. Jesus Christ himself*
> *hymned with a voice purer than that of the angels his song*
> *of obedience when, after he had partaken of the Last Supper,*
> *he went with his disciples to Gethsemane.*

'*Thus it is fitting to say before this altar: honour, blessing and gratitude to the artists, the pious men who, endowed with the great gift of being able to lift souls above worldly things through harmony, regard themselves as offering sacrifice to the living God.*

'*God wants you to think and work with the remembrance of him ever present to you. Dearly beloved brother, first and foremost you must use your genius to influence beneficially the soul of your young wife. In giving her to you, God expects you to help her to become worthy of eternal life. Accept and fulfil this task in the ardent wish that you may offer her to him at the last, clothed in the true bridal raiment which is the Justice of the Saints.*

'*Beloved sister, daughter of this Church, the God of your fathers wishes to be your God and your counsellor throughout your entire life. For you, sacred and revered memories hover around this altar and these are such as to enlighten and strengthen your youthful conscience. Your grandfather and your father gave out the bread of life in this church and offered prayers and hymns to the sovereign Judge and benefactor of all men. These Christian thoughts still have power to stir those among us who enjoyed the benefits of their ministry and who to-day call down blessings from Heaven upon you in their memory.*

'*When you received instruction before your Confirmation, and during your Communions, you, yourself, dear sister, were aware of these beneficent influences upon you. In making yourself one with God through Jesus Christ, you were able to join with gladness the other members of your family.*

'*May you put on the incorruptible purity of a tranquil and gentle heart which is of great value in the eyes of God!*

'*But I hope that a blessed voice may join with mine in reminding you both how your marriage may fulfil its eternal purpose! This voice will be that of your Father, beloved sister—and in this way the Gospel truth will be proved for you that "after his death his word liveth on".*'

Ferdinand Hiller wrote: 'It was extraordinary to hear so fundamentally German an artist express himself in French at this solemn moment. The simplicity of the ceremony and the young couple who were so attractive in every way combined to captivate and move every heart.'

The French Church in Frankfurt.
Organ and gallery.

After the service, whose beauty was enhanced by floral decorations and a fine concert, the French Church was emptied of all the personages who had come there to meditate—senators of the town among them. The flood of faithful parishioners—the Mendelssohn Bartholdys, the Jeanrenauds, the Souchays, the Perrets, the de Neufvilles, the Le Jeunes, the Bethmanns, Rohmer, the de Barys, Osterrieth, de Bihl, de Loën, Baumhauer, Le Long, Schunck, Schlemmer, Jordis, du Fay, Gontard,

*Decorations in a corner of the large salon of the Souchay's house in Frankfurt
in 1837.*

It was in this room that the wedding breakfast was held on March 28th.

d'Orville, du Bosc, Passavant, Sarasin, Bernus, Rapin, de
Famars, Textor, de Flamerdingue—all this elegant procession
wended its way in carriages back to the Fahrthor.

The reception was held in this ancient dwelling of the Souchays and dinner was served on the first floor, in a large room
with five windows looking out on to the Main. The room was

richly decorated with panelling in the Renaissance style, ornamented with statues, classical silhouettes in relief, garlands, cups and masks, and it was here, before the guests and the busy servants, that a choir of ladies assembled by Hiller arrayed themselves to perform his *Wedding Song*, composed especially for the occasion. But the rather martial lines of singers broke and there were smiles on every face when the happy bride and bridegroom made their entrance with their retinue.

Was it not Lamartine who said? ... 'Il y a de ces êtres qui rayonnent, qui éblouissent, qui entraînent tout dans leur sphère d'attraction autour d'eux sans y penser, sans le vouloir, sans le savoir même. On dirait que certaines natures ont un système comme les astres et font graviter les regards, les âmes et les pensées de leurs satellites dans leur propre mouvement. La beauté physique ou morale est leur puissance, la fascination est leur chaîne, l'amour est leur émanation.'

Surely it would be surprising if two brilliant spirits such as Felix and Cécile, distinct from each other and yet alike, thrown together in the world, did not have an attraction one for the other? Two forces, in appearance poles apart, were from that time on united. Two striking personalities, remarkable for their analogous conceptions of the dignity of life, alike in their love of poetry, both convinced that there is neither religion without sacrifice nor greatness without faith, were to keep their vows given before God and man—and that, in the absorbing stories of artists' lives is a rare occurrence.

VII

A HONEYMOON JOURNEY

The atmosphere of warmth and love which surrounded the
marriage of Felix and Cécile Mendelssohn Bartholdy can to-day
be re-created from the diaries kept by members of their circle,
a few private notes, and the letters which they exchanged with
close relatives and scattered friends. Their own letters, those
which they addressed to each other throughout their lives, were
all burned at a later date. The composer and his wife did not
wish to make this personal correspondence public. However,
their letters to relatives and friends remain. Cecile's, though
preserved, were not until recently known to exist. The majority
of the letters written by Felix were published by his two sons.
In addition, there is the diary which they kept during their
honeymoon; the writing is mostly by Cécile and the illustrations
are by Felix.

Mendelssohn's biographers speak of four journeys made by
the composer; two before his marriage—in 1822, at the age of
13, and in 1831, at the age of 22—two after his marriage—in
1842 and 1847. Apart from his frequent trips to and from England, there was a fifth journey, between the two first and the
two last. The young couple left an entertaining account, in the
form of a diary, of their travels during their honeymoon.

Ask a newly-wed couple, very much in love, what they saw
in a town which they visited on their honeymoon. You will
discover that they saw nothing. It would be most unfair to
question two lovers on the glories of Rome, and a great mistake
to turn the conversation on to the beauties of the Adriatic. Put
them in some wretched plot of countryside; that is where they

would just as soon make their journey round the world! At the
time when Toepffer was recounting his charming 'Zigzag Journeys', Felix and Cécile were wandering about the Upper Rhineland and Swabia. That Worms is a town of historical interest, in

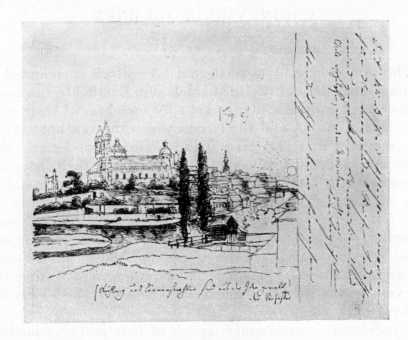

Spires Cathedral.
Drawing by Mendelssohn.

which Luther laid his theses before the Imperial Diet, that it
contains a magnificent Roman church, tombs, monuments, all
full of interest—of these facts the two lovers do not breathe a
word. At that time, Luther's statue had not yet been erected on
its site in the centre of the city, where it stands surrounded by a
forest of great personalities—his precursors, Huss, Savonarola,
Wyclif, Pierre de Vaux, Philip the Magnanimous of Hesse,
Frederick the Wise, Melanchthon, and Reuchlin. But if, ignoring
the anachronism, you had asked the two lovers what they thought

of this statue by Rietschel, they would no doubt have replied that it was excellent.

They stayed a few days at Spires, centre of the Bavarian Rhineland, and there, Felix, whose musical spirits were beginning

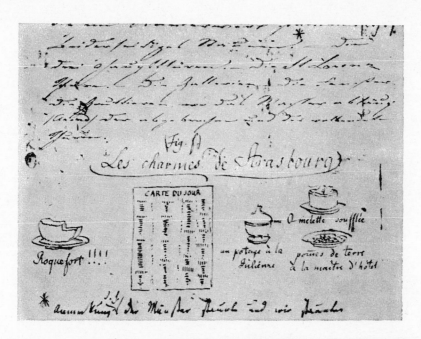

'Menu' ... or the charms of Strasbourg.
Drawing by Mendelssohn.

to revive, composed three organ preludes, as well as drawing the cathedral which for 800 years had stood on the height above the town. The day before, having inspected the clock and the bells, they climbed one of the towers. Cécile, for the first time in her life, was giddy ... Mendelssohn included in his drawing an impressionistic Louis XIV sun setting on the horizon.

This same sun may have watched over a certain memorable day in Frankfurt and described wonderful parabolas in the sky above Spires; but cold and snow accompanied our travellers as far as Strasbourg. There, soon after the flight of a mass of heavy, galloping clouds, the old French city blossomed beneath a blue sky. The transept, chancel, and crypt, the ogives and sculptures of its spired cathedral rising to dominate the vista of Vosges

Lunch in Strasbourg, Monsieur Berg's entrance.
Drawing by Mendelssohn.

mountains and Black Forest, held the interest of Felix and Cécile. Amused, they watched the animation of the Broglie. At the Opera, they disappeared after the first act. Was the music bad? Did they want to kiss? No information is supplied on this point. The evening concluded with a tasty supper. The foie gras of which the people of Strasbourg are so proud is noticeably absent from the menu. The supper consisted of julienne soup, potatoes '*à la maître d'hôtel*', Roquefort, and omelette soufflée. A certain Monsieur Berg (see drawing), a strange and importunate person armed with an umbrella, disturbed the newly-wed couple in their apparently diligent reading of the newspapers.

On a fine April morning, Cécile entered a dressmaker's shop in the gay city on the Ill. Mme Piqué's was a very popular shop;

Charming display at the milliner's.
Drawing by Mendelssohn.

its drawers abounded with gloves and scarves and smart hats; its shelves were piled with rolls of elegant cloth. Felix listened to the conversation from the doorway. In the 'Hochzeitstagebuch', Cécile noted in French the affable greeting of the woman behind the counter: 'Madam, you ought to take this ribbon with the little green buds. It's just the thing for spring, it's lovely!'

A walk along the banks of the leaping river Dreisam brought the lovers through fields strewn with primroses to the whirling wheels of a paper factory; close by, in the green meadow, there

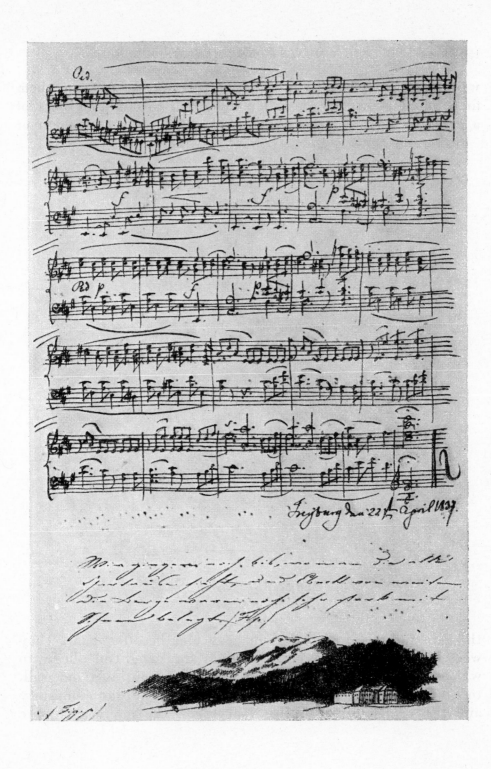

were charming processions of violets. 'It was I who saw them first, and I picked all those I could reach through the bars of a gate. They were for his buttonhole. But Felix climbed over

Paper-mill near Freiburg im Breisgau.
Drawing by Mendelssohn.

the gate and gathered little bunches which he offered me. They were exquisite, but no more so than the delightful allegretto which he composed for me on this theme. We continued our walk to a spot from which we could see the old Carthusian monastery and the village of Ebenach. Near them, the mountains were covered with snow.' Felix drew this gate over which he had climbed; it can be seen behind the two tumbledown cottages.

Another trip took them to the Carthusian monastery of

Spring posy.
Drawing by Cécile Mendelssohn.

Ebenach, of which there is a sketch underneath the allegretto. On their return, Felix added roses and hyacinths to a freshly-gathered bunch of violets. Throughout the night and the following day, these delicate flowers scented their room. Cécile sentimentally pressed the flowers into her album.

In a letter to his sister, Felix wrote that he could scarcely describe how blissfully happy he was; composing quartets in the morning, while Cécile painted, walking with her in the sunshine, making plans for the summer, finishing his songs without words so as to be able to begin more important compositions, and doing everything with enthusiasm.

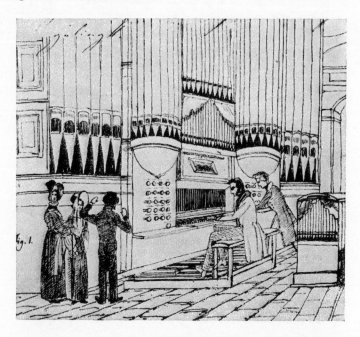

At the organ in Heidelberg. Church of the Holy Ghost.
Drawing by Mendelssohn.

After the 3rd of May, they made trips to Todtnau, Mambach, Zell, Schopfheim, and Lorrach, stopping at Freiburg im Breisgau. From the hill of the Schlossberg, they had a view of the smiling valley of the Dreisam. In the streets of Freiburg, the waters of the river flowed in clear streams.

A coach which rolled along lines of ruts brought them to Rastaft. They halted at this old city, with its hill and its castle, and afterwards once again at Heidelberg. In the ancient capital of the Palatinate, they climbed over the ruins of the castle. Did they not have to admire the masterpieces of Renaissance sculpture, the gate carved with caryatids, the biblical statues of Collins de Malines? Their next visits were to relatives, the Souchays, the Fallensteins, and the Webers; and at Heidelberg, too, Cécile had the pleasant surprise of seeing and embracing her mother.

Thicket near Saxenhausen.
Drawing by Mendelssohn

On the 8th of May they ... wandered about among the passageways of the building which proudly showed its gigantic barrel to all comers. A master brewer—a wit, in his own way?—performed the ritual ceremony of giving each visitor three taps on the backside with an enormous wooden knife. They ran to escape a freak storm which poured down on the city of the Neckar; and a gallop was the proper pace at which to go to meet, in the Church of the Holy Spirit, that old friend and cousin of Cécile's, Fritz Schlemmer who, had been to some extent responsible for the happy ceremony which they had so recently celebrated. He gave the young couple a veritable organ concert. On the following days, while the rain continued, Mendelssohn and Schlemmer spent long hours at the organ. A sketch shows the two musicians improvising, making the vaults of the empty church resound with austere fugues. In addition, Felix was composing all the time. During his honeymoon journey, he produced, among other works, Psalm Op. 42, for choir, solos, and orchestra.

Darmstadt was the next stop. The two occasional artists were able to savour its rich collection of paintings; works by Rembrandt—a Christ on a pillar—Nymphs and Satyrs by Rubens, and canvases by Fabritius and van der Neer, Holbein and Annibal Carrache. Having left the distinguished capital and court residence of Hesse, Felix and Cécile were bumped along towards Frankfurt in the traditional noisy, rattling stage-coach, with the driver's whip cracking over the tandem-driven horses.

From Frankfurt, the honeymoon journey began afresh. The diary contains two drawings, dated the 26th of May, the first of which, by Felix, represents the luxuriant low wood of Oberad. A flower-bed aroused their delight, displaying a blue carpet of paludous myosotis—botanical name for the flower called 'forget-me-not, remember-me, the-more-I-see-you-the-more-I-love-you'. They got down from their carriage, and while the coachman restrained his impatient horses on the road, Cécile and Felix ran into the forest and gathered large bunches of these charming flowers. Were they not keeping an appointment with the young lovers and whispering in their ear: the more I see you, the more I love you? 'We filled the whole of my sunshade with these lovely little blue flowers'.

At Kreutznach, a resort well known for its brine baths, Felix and Cécile spent the afternoon of the 9th August, 1837. Near the Nahe Bridge was the watering station, with its rather primitive hotels and its already very fashionable casino. The main ball-room and its galleries and colonnades were decorated with green

Dance at the Kreutznach Casino.
Drawing by Mendelssohn

garlands. Elegant patrons of the baths, bewhiskered, tightly trousered, and smiling, whirled through giddy polkas and open mazurkas in treble time with stout, full-bosomed ladies, their hair piled up in monumental chignons, and wearing crinolines and lace from France or England. By a tacit agreement, the very old and the very young watched, soberly and wonderingly, from picturesque benches. With a few witty strokes of his pen, Felix accurately and delightfully reproduces the pleasant atmosphere of this fashionable dance. No doubt he too, excellent dancer as he was, led his young wife through a few accomplished movements and *entrechats*, amid the general rustling of silk and bowing of invitations.

The young couple stayed for a short time in Frankfurt. Their temporary residence in that town was the last episode in their voyage of discovery, a fairy-tale journey of unforgettable happiness. The manuscript finishes appropriately; for a maestro as famous as Mendelssohn could not for long stand aside from the musical impulse which he gave to the whole of Europe. Although Felix, since his marriage, had sought to avoid the turbulent public concerts which excited and exhausted him, he had, nevertheless, to resume his routine to some extent. On the 24th of August, he decided hurriedly on a cross-Channel journey, so as to conduct Händel's *Solomon* and his own famous *Saint Paul* in Birmingham; his oratorio aroused immense enthusiasm.

At Frankfurt, Cécile continued their little honeymoon manuscript alone. Opposite each of her notes, she left an empty space on a second sheet of paper; so that Felix, on his return, could relate what had happened to him. On the 27th of September she wrote: 'I am sitting here, waiting. It is now half past eleven. Since waking up this morning, I have been listening to every sound in the house. How disappointed I am! Felix is not yet here!'

On the space which she had left blank in the album, Mendelssohn later wrote: 'I was on the Rhine and woke up at half past two. Was the boat going to stop unexpectedly? It did, in fact, stop. There was a thick fog over the countryside. Faced with this obstacle, we had to remain where we were all night. The captain hoped to start up again early in the morning, so as to get to Mainz at about six o'clock. I immediately recognised Pfaffendorf. It was a curious fact that I should have slept for several hours not far from my dear uncle's house[1]. Deciding to leave the boat, I got two sailors to carry my luggage and hurried along the path which borders the Rhine as far as Ehrenbreitstein. Just as I was passing the bridge where, two months ago, I used so often to walk with Cécile, the clock in the convent struck three. I jumped into a carriage, and an hour later was on my way to Boppard. The boat was far behind me. Every minute, passing through villages where I had so recently been in the company of my dear wife, I grew more impatient to see her again. Boppard! There was the inn where we used to dine together. At five o'clock, St. Goar! The inn-keeper told me that Cécile and her mother had recently passed through. At Baccara, memories faced me everywhere. Just before Niederwald, the fog lifted. At Bingen, the sun came out. Ah! I caught a glimpse of the teacher who offered me his piano. Behind me, black fog; in front, bright sunshine! At midday we passed through Mainz. It was half past two when I saw Frankfurt ... I ran through its familiar streets. My absence was over! Happily, I kissed my beloved Cécile.'

---

[1] Georges-Benjamin Mendelssohn, 1794 - 1874—son of Joseph and grandson of the philosopher Moses Mendelssohn—married to Rosemonde Richter, lived at Horchheim. He had been a professor at Bonn. Felix retained happy memories of the holidays which he had spent with him as a child. Benjamin Mendelssohn had no children. His branch of the family was continued by his brother, Alexander, who had daughters and three sons, one of whom was Franz von Mendelssohn, president of the International Chamber of Commerce; there are living descendants of all three sons of Alexander.

Felix Mendelssohn Bartholdy.
A painting attributed to Edouard Magnus,
the property of M. Robert Bory, Coppet.

VIII

THE HOME

On the 1st October, 1837, Felix and Cécile arrived in Leipzig, which was to be their home. Five days later, the young husband wrote to his brother-in-law, Charles Jeanrenaud, who had just obtained a doctorate in law and was on the point of entering practice as a lawyer:

'I feel I must tell you of the adaptability which your sister has shown in her new surroundings. Within a few days she has succeeded in giving our home, from which I am now writing, a most agreeable and comfortable appearance. We are glad that the moving in will be complete in four weeks; then, we shall arrange things to our taste and we shall be very satisfied. Everything will look beautiful. Cécile is coping with the builders and furnishers. She is buying fruit-dishes, salad-bowls, knives, and forks... While she is doing this, I am busy with music-publishers, touring virtuosi, and cantatrices. If the public is as enthusiastic as Cécile, I shall have no cause to worry! Never have my meals seemed so tasty.'

Seeking for a means of helping his brother-in-law, Felix informed Charles that he was recommending him to municipal councillors and chambers of commerce. A short while afterwards, he offered to provide Charles with references from the banking houses Mendelssohn & Co., of Berlin, and Paul Mendelssohn Bartholdy of Hamburg.

Husband and wife, as will be seen later, were not always to share their duties in the picturesque way described in Mendelssohn's letter. Not that dishes and bowls and good cutlery are an insecure basis for the domestic life of a famous composer;

it is a grave error to suppose that those who lack genius are likely to acquire it through hunger!

During the year 1837, most members of the Mendelssohn Bartholdy family made the acquaintance of the composer's wife. A century ago, however, distances were of greater importance than to-day. Felix had many times to postpone his journey to Berlin, though Fanny Hensel was longing to receive, with tender affection, the wife her brother had chosen.

'I must say', she wrote to her sister-in-law, 'that you have both been very naughty. Not so much as a line to tell us about your moving to Leipzig!

'If Felix, after all the recent excitement, has at last entered a period of tranquillity, it is you whom we must thank, my dear Cécile. The agitation of his public life worries me, even in my quiet little backwater. I am very curious to know how his Concerto was received. When a work by Felix reaches me for the first time in print, I judge it just as the public does, without any favourable bias. But I think back with regret to those happy times when Felix took me into his confidence, step by step, as the inspiration awoke in him. How strange and vexing it is that we should all live so far apart, and that after six months of marriage I should still not know my brother's wife. I am no longer willing to listen to accounts of your beauty, and I get quite annoyed when people speak to me about your eyes—it is time I could admire those charming eyes myself!'

When, a little while later, Mme Hensel paid a visit to Leipzig, she found Cécile not only as exquisitely beautiful as description had painted her, but also endowed with qualities of character which she hastened to praise:

'A weight has been lifted from me since I made the acquaintance of my sister-in-law. I had been growing impatient on account of our prolonged separation. She is so charming, so full of spontaneity and freshness of feeling, and at the same time so gentle and sincere, that I can only congratulate Felix on his choice. Cécile loves him deeply, but does not spoil him overmuch.

She brings to their relationship an evenness of temper which will finally stabilise the more capricious nature of Felix.'

Another letter shows that Mme Hensel had produced an equally favourable impression on Cécile:

'I have been very much moved by all the kind things you have said to me, my dear Cécile. I do not think I have ever wanted to please anyone as much as I have wanted to please you. Your kind assurances lead me to hope that I have succeeded. But you know that in order to judge a woman, you have to see her in her own home, and you will not know me properly until after your visit to Berlin. I am sure that you will feel perfectly at home. How glad we shall all be to see him again!'

Mendelssohn's charming younger sister, the wife of Gustave Dirichlet (a well-known mathematician, at that time Professor at the Military School, Berlin University, and whose remarkable work was later to be published under the auspices of the university) reveals, in a few lines written to Julie Jeanrenaud on the 26th of September 1837, something of those conflicts of affection which marriages so often arouse:

'Please do not say too harshly that Felix has taken your sister away from you. I know from experience how, at the beginning, one hates one's brother-in-law; but on this occasion you have gained a very good brother. . . I call him good, although I should be angry with him for not letting me come and kiss my new sister in Frankfurt!'

Felix, for his part, in letters to his friend Edouard Devrient —one of a family of French refugees in Germany—conveys the same impression of beneficent tranquillity resulting from his recent marriage. Edouard Devrient (whose uncle, keystone of the German theatre of his time, was called the German Garrick, as a tribute to his rendering in all their primitive force of Lear, Macbeth, Richard III—outcast of nature—and Shylock—outcast of society) was prominent in the musical world as a baritone of brilliant repute. His two brothers and their wives—one of them a daughter of the famous Schroeder—were actors of a high order, and played throughout Germany in the dramas of Schiller and Goethe. Edouard Devrient wrote of Cécile: 'She spoke little. Shakespeare would have called her, "sweet silence".'

The Thomasschule in Leipzig, about 1840.
Drawing by Mendelssohn Bartholdy.

Mendelssohn's immense happiness, the sort of recrudescent joy which he experienced in living beside his young wife in the charming, cosy home which she had built up, mingled with the rhythm of his musical activity. He continued to work incessantly at compositions which filled his days to overflowing, but he wrote: 'How delightful and easy it is to work, how happy I am!'

If, in his private life, Mendelssohn Bartholdy was feeling a

wonderful wellbeing, living between his music and his young
wife, composing uninterruptedly, and completing a forthcoming
oratorio, he was, with equal felicity, in his public life, maintaining

Part of the home of Mendelssohn Bartholdy in Leipzig.
Watercolour by Felix completed by Cécile;
the property of the Wach family, Wilderswil.

the renown of Leipzig, pre-eminent capital in the realm of music.
Though he might have maintained this renown solely with his own
compositions, he avoided imposing them on his programmes.
Always the work of other composers — often rivals — was given
pride of place: Bach, Händel, Gluck, Haydn, Mozart, Schubert,
Weber, Cimarosa, Salieri, Berlioz, Beethoven, Schumann, and
later Wagner.

Mendelssohn found relaxation from his duties as director of the Gewandhaus, in drawing the Thomasschule, or the house in which he lived, with its surrounding garden. But above all he was absorbed in his own musical compositions, wherein he could exercise in all their glory his amazing stylistic talents. Meanwhile, painting in oils became increasingly Cécile's main recreation, and one which she undertook with ease and assurance. Their individual tastes contrasted with those of the Hensels, where the husband painted and the wife composed. 'Your marriage', Fanny Hensel remarked, 'is the double counterpoint of ours!'

In 1838, there was a small family reunion to witness the baptism of Cécile's firstborn; Felix's brother, Paul, was present, with his wife, Albertine Heine, as well as Madame Jeanrenaud and her daughter, Julie, who brought the good wishes of M. Appia and the news of the death of Auguste Touchon. Charles Jeanrenaud and Paul Mendelssohn Bartholdy were godfathers to the baby, about whom Cécile, a few days later, sent the following note to her brother: 'He is very much like you, with dark hair and dark blue eyes; he gurgles comfortably when he is asleep! I was very pleased to receive the news you sent about M. Bernus.'

Little Carl now gave the house in Leipzig the wonderfully human animation of a family home—that environment despised on principle by so many false artists and snobs, who imagine that the supreme expression of art and genius is aroused only by libertinage or misfortune. After Felix had amused himself painting in his studio, with its white muslin curtains against the blue wallpaper, its brown couch and gay carpeted floor, his wife, knowing that he had gone off to a rehearsal, would take up the brush and quickly add a few necessary touches to the water-colour ... she herself working in a corner of the studio, while little Carl pulled a toy sheep round the room at the end of a piece of string. On his return, it is said, Felix used to grumble at the completion of his rough sketch.

In the summer of 1838, Felix, Cécile, and young Carl were joyously welcomed in Berlin by the family, who had at this time much cause for satisfaction. Just before the coronation, Hensel's painting 'Miriam', had been bought by Queen Victoria, after the queen, wishing to admire his work fully, had herself designated the Buckingham Gallery as an exhibition hall for his paintings. The Duke of Egerton had suggested to him as a subject, 'Brunswick at a ball in Brussels, while the guns of Waterloo are firing.' The Duchess of Sutherland had also given Cécile's brother-in-law a commission. Hensel, like Felix, was on the road to fame[1]. Cécile became more intimately acquainted with her husband's family. They entertained in her honour, they spoiled her, and as a member of their circle her taste for the arts developed.

Felix was extraordinarily busy; but henceforth he was able to refresh himself in the salutary calm and restfulness of his own home. In May 1838 he directed the Cologne festival, and then began his Leipzig concerts once more.

Meanwhile, Hensel and Fanny wrote from Venice:

'We have just seen the studio of the painter Nerly, which I wanted specially to visit because it was there that Leopold Robert committed suicide. It was a moving experience for me to set foot in the same room, to climb the same staircase; we had vividly before us the memory of all the details of his life and his death.' In 1835, the famous Neuchâtel painter, Leopold Robert, had cut his throat with a razor, after having fallen desperately in love with the princess Charlotte Bonaparte, a niece of Napoleon the First and daughter of Joseph, King of Naples. 'To finish our round of visits that morning, we called

---

[1] William Hensel, born in 1794, fought as a volunteer in the war of independence. On his return, his drawing showed talent, and he illustrated many almanacs. During five years of study in Italy, fascinated by the works of the great Italian masters, he painted in Rome 'Jesus Christ and the Samaritan Woman' and 'Victoria Caldoni at the fountain'. In 1828, he settled in Berlin as professor at the Academy of Art and painter to the king and the court. He began, in 1848, a masterly collection of portraits of famous contemporaries. His success in England too was considerable. Queen Victoria received, honoured, and encouraged him. There are numerous portraits by Hensel of his brother-in-law, Felix Mendelssohn. Hensel's sisters, Louisa (died 1876) and Wilhelmina (died 1893), wrote a delightful collection of German poems, published in 1858 by Kletke. Wilhelm Hensel, who lost his wife, Fanny Mendelssohn Bartholdy, in 1847, died in Berlin on the 26th of November, 1861.

on Aurèle Robert, who still lives in the flat—the studio is not in
the same building—which he shared till the end with his brother.
We received a final impression of this moving tragedy. Aurèle
showed us drawings made for his brother's paintings, as well as
other sketches'. The Hensels lived for a time in the same house
as Aurèle Robert, who was a compatriot of their sister-in-law,
Cécile Jeanrenaud. They referred admiringly to Aurèle's paintings and to those of his dead brother, Leopold. They liked
equally their paintings in the genre 'Campagna Shepherd'—'a
landscape of sheep and men'—and their renderings of the
'Madonna of the Arch' festival, at which the Hensels themselves
were present in 1840, among wagons loaded with green branches,
to the sound of tambourines and castanets, in a completely
romantic procession of revellers, 'like a fresco motif'. Fanny also
praised highly another Neuchâtel painter, Alexandre Calame,
who excelled in the quite different genre of Alpine landscapes.

At Christmas 1839, sending greetings to her sister-in-law
Jeanne Jeanrenaud-de Bihl, in Frankfurt, Cécile described her
home, full of presents and decorations, and glittering with
candles, in front of which her fascinated son sat on a rocking-
horse, urging it on with coachman's cries. Hiller had an elegant
set of crystal flower-vases sent from Frankfurt as a gift to his
friends. A charming set of shelves was filled with 'all my little
porcelain dolls'.

During the first months of 1840, Felix gave some ten public
performances. 'I had worked beforehand for eight days without
a break. I could no longer remain standing, and I walked along
the street in "organ passages".' In August of the following year,
Mendelssohn Bartholdy, the Lutheran, revived in Leipzig the
work of Germany's greatest protestant musician: Johann Sebastian Bach. He arranged a performance in the Church of
St. Thomas of *St. Matthew's Passion*, which had not been heard
there for 110 years. This tenacity and determined preference in
taste were characteristic of Felix, who, having already revealed
Bach to the Singakademie and to Berlin in 1829, now presented

Bach once again, in 1841, this time to the whole of Germany. By honouring the great musician in the native land which had forgotten him—in Leipzig itself, from which brilliant rays of light had dazzled the continent—Felix lit a powerful flame, a torch which shines to-day above all the light and all the darkness.

The picture which we have of Mendelssohn at this period is an unvarying one, perhaps because, man of genius that he was, he did not attitudinize. The mobility of his facial expression was based on an unchanging certainty of character, the same in the publicity of the concert-hall as in the privacy of his home. His complexion was fresh and lightly coloured. Above a high forehead grew an abundance of fine black hair, which, towards the end of his life, was threaded with silver. A circle of short black beard set off his remarkably distinguished profile. The darkness and strength of his beard gave a blueish tinge to his shaven chin and upper lip. His expressive mouth, with lips drawn back in a smile, surrounded fine, regular white teeth. In moments of emotion, or when he was improvising, his dark eyes shone and sparkled with intensity. Among friends, he was so inclined to laughter, that at times he would literally twist up and wave his hand in a characteristic gesture, emphasising his expression of uncontrollable gaiety. His highly developed sense of comedy and humour made him particularly popular among the English. The elegance of his build was in keeping with his facial expressiveness. His slender fingers danced on the keys with such ease, such intelligence, that they seemed to be animated with an independent, prodigious life of their own. Yet seated at the piano, he showed no affectation. At the organ, he sometimes bent very low over the keyboard, as though wishing to listen more attentively to the winged melodies born of his will. His playing was calm and fascinating. Unrivalled among orchestral conductors, he was loved and feared; no fault escaped his ear. Schumann, Berlioz, and many others gave him their unreserved admiration. He aroused no enmity, scarcely even jealousy, though any sign of meanness and deceit evoked his righteous indignation.

Robert and Clara Schumann.
Universal-Edition, Vienna.

He was in no way effeminate or morbid. His qualities, which harmonised so well with those of his wife, were modesty, piety, courtesy—and genius.

'Cilette', as Fanny Hensel called her, cleverly guided the threads of conversation, whether as hostess or guest, rather than herself initiating them. In musical matters, Felix continually submitted his ideas to her, asked advice, played over his themes. Such was always their practice. Senator Souchay noted in his diary:

'Cécile took an active part in his work and assisted its progress. She received, on his behalf, the numerous admirers and musicians recommended to him. No one went away dissatisfied, because she was exquisite to look at. In her interviews with these gentlemen, rather than display her intelligence, she allowed them to guess at it; they preferred that!'

Clearly, Cécile was not the sort of artist's wife whose interests are confined to serving tea! There was in the Mendelssohn Bartholdy household, thanks to Cécile Jeanrenaud—a Madonna by Raphael—an enchanted atmosphere of delightful warmth and exquisite happiness.

Such friends as Robert and Clara Schumann, and Hiller, were frequent visitors to their idyllic family circle; which was enlarged, in 1839, by the birth of a daughter, Marie—to whom Carl, the elder, passed on the string lead of his toy sheep on wheels... 'Little Carl delighted us by the way he spoke and opened his mouth to express himself in German. Various relatives of his mother came and went. It was a most happy occasion, a gathering of pleasant circumstances such as chance brings together for few people so completely. How heartily we laughed one day when Cécile, returning from the Gewandhaus where she had listened to the concert among the audience, told how she had heard a few women nearby commiserating with her feelingly on the inhuman, cruel, and barbaric way in which Felix treated her.' Hiller adds humorously: 'Nothing really merits the sympathy of an audience so full of pity.'

On another occasion, Felix and Cécile sat among the audience during a concert of works by Hiller. 'Felix told me that his enjoyment of my music had been heightened by the extremely expert opinions of his wife, whose appreciation and judgement were always full of wisdom.'

Each year, on her birthday, Cécile entertained a crowd of relatives, both from the Jeanrenaud and Mendelssohn Bartholdy sides of her family. These were gay reunions which strengthened her feeling for the family as a comfort and a holy basis for peace of spirit.

In 1840 began the reign of Frederick William IV. This sovereign was reluctant to admit that in the development of the arts Berlin was surpassed, and far surpassed, by other German cities. Not content with having reorganised the Academy, he called to the rescue of the capital numerous outstanding men of his kingdom. He offered Felix, through his brother Paul, the post of director of music in a revivified Academy of the Arts. His plan was to found a Conservatoire and to organize first-rate concerts with the assistance of artists of the royal theatre. Although nominated by the king and encouraged by his relatives, who wanted to have him near them in Berlin, Mendelssohn needed a great deal of persuading.

The offer of an attractive salary did not tempt him. But after persuasion from many quarters, he accepted the new post provisionally, retaining meanwhile his flat in Leipzig. Shortly afterwards, in January 1841, Cécile gave birth in Leipzig to a son, Paul. 'My third child is a pretty little lamb. I can't believe I have been married for four years.' Mendelssohn and his family then moved for a time to Berlin. Cécile was far from displeased by the change of surroundings. Her painter's eye was delighted by the masses of hyacinths and tulips in many colours blooming beside the flowering cherry-trees, pear-trees, peach-trees, and almond-trees of the magnificent Mendelssohn Bartholdy garden. Moreover, she could never be bored in Berlin. She had already written, in April of the previous year, during a stay in the town:

Frederick William IV.

King of Prussia and patron of the great Mendelssohn.
From a lithograph by E. Meyer.

'We find the time here passing most agreeably. We go to the theatre often, which we cannot do in Leipzig. The opera is almost as beautiful as in Milan. The performances—especially those of Spontini, which he conducts himself—show such brilliance that one is quite overwhelmed by the mass of sound and dazzled by its glitter. The king likes that very much. Although he is said to be very ill, he has himself carried to the theatre. Mysterious rumours are being spread about, and prophecies which disturb His Majesty. They say that bells toll in the castle without anybody ringing them. They say, also, that his minister, Altenstein, is dying.' Altenstein and the king did, in fact, die not long afterwards, the latter on Whit Sunday.

It was during her stay in Berlin that Cécile sat for Edward Magnus, that extraordinary magician of portraiture. Born in Berlin in 1799, he had not taken up painting until the age of 23. In Rome, his scenes of popular life very soon brought him celebrity. Portraits which assure his fame are those of Thorwaldsen, Jenny Lind, Countess Rossi, Felix Mendelssohn Bartholdy, Cécile, the Empress Augusta, and Count Wrangel. Magnus, a member of the Senate of the Academy of Berlin, died in 1872. At the time when he was painting Cécile's portrait, the young couple, ideally married and still very much in love, were the subject of much conversation in the capital, where they had made a lively and popular impression.

The work which Felix undertook in Berlin, in 1841, under the new king, aroused in him scarcely anything but bitter feelings. He accused Liszt of continually and deliberately clowning. And on top of everything, he was greatly overworked. 'Since January, I have given fifteen public performances, enough to kill any man!' During this crowded period, when he was in addition Kapellmeister to the king of Saxony, to whom he had promised to give concerts in Dresden, Felix no longer found the necessary leisure in which to compose. The pure development of his musical genius suffered. He was scarcely able to enjoy his customary sense of complete calm beside his wife.

Although, out of deference to Frederick William IV, Mendelssohn had consented to remain the king's composer, he none the less decided to move his home from Berlin and make his head-quarters once again in Leipzig, to which he had already return-ed several times to conduct concerts. He wanted to recapture the peace of his dear Gewandhaus, in which he finally completed the Scottish Sym-phony. Meanwhile, at the unveiling of a mo-nument to Bach, he had been awarded the title of 'Citizen of Leip-zig'.

Queen Victoria and Prince Albert.
From 'Queen Victoria'
by Abel Chevalley (Delagrave, Paris).

In the spring of 1842, he made a trip to England and receiv-ed immense ovations. Queen Victoria's ent-husiasm for his work was such that she au-thorised the personal dedication to her of the Scottish Symphony. He played many times in private at Buckingham Palace. 'Grahl claims that Buckingham Palace is the only house in England where one is put completely at one's ease, after having received the kindest hospitality.

Ball at 'La Grenette', Lausanne, given by the Swiss Society of Music, the 4th of August, 1842.
Drawing by Bonnet and engraving by Bryner.
The property of M. Georges-A. Bridel.

Joking apart, Prince Albert invited me to spend Saturday with him in order to try his organ. I found him alone in his library; hardly had the conversation begun, when the queen appeared, wearing a dressing-gown and ready to leave an hour later for Claremont. "Heavens! How untidy!" she cried, seeing sheets of a score scattered over the floor. She immediately knelt down to pick them up. Prince Albert followed her example and I hastened to do the same, but the queen assured us that she could pick them up alone.

'At my request, the prince sat at the organ and played by heart a chorale, with a purity and expressiveness that many another organist might envy. The queen, having finished what she was doing, came over to her husband and followed his playing with perceptible satisfaction. For my part, I played a chorale from "Paulus"; the king and queen sang the chorus with me. The queen then proposed singing a tune by Glück. We went to her rooms, where, in her boudoir, there was a piano, and beside it a large rocking-horse and two enormous cages. Turning over some music, I discovered my first collection of songs and asked Her Majesty to sing a Lied, in preference to a tune by Glück. She consented most graciously and sang—guess what?— *Schöner und schöner*, which she rendered very charmingly, with a correct feeling for the time and the expression. I confessed that this song was by Fanny and asked the queen to sing one of mine. "If you will help me a little, I will do so gladly", she replied. Her Majesty then sang without the least hesitation and with much feeling, my Lied: *Lass' dich nur nichts dauern.* I thanked her effusively, but thought it more fitting not to give praise. The queen excused herself: "My feelings were too strong and I could not sustain my notes as usual. I have generally more breath". This time I protested and expressed my admiration freely.

'The prince also sang, and then asked me to develop on the piano the theme which he had played on the organ and the theme of his song. I obeyed with a certain amount of uneasiness. Would my improvisations come up to their expectations ? But everything combined that day to produce a favourable impression. I added the themes of the lieder sung by the queen to the themes which had been asked for, and I improvised to my heart's content.

Hector Berlioz.
Universal-Edition, Vienna.

The intelligent attention given to me by Her Majesty and the prince stimulated my inspiration. I had the feeling of having done good work. When I had finished, the queen made me promise to come back soon to England. A quarter of an hour later, the palace flag was lowered and the papers announced: "Her Majesty left the palace at half-past three" ... After this description, let Dirichlet try calling me an aristocrat again! Wasn't I more radical than ever ?'

Mendelssohn's letter shows, not only the artist's modesty and his pleasure in being understood, but also a complete absence of the spirit of flattery or intrigue. It opens a simple window on to the generous soul of a superior artist, a distinguished German honoured and intimately received by a great queen.

In August 1842, Cécile, Felix, his brother Paul, and the latter's wife Albertine, travelled about Switzerland; a pleasant relaxation after the performance of the *Lobgesang*, conducted at Düsseldorf. From Interlaken they set out on numerous trips. At Meiringen, the composer met his guide, Michel again. The four friends, transformed for the time being into keen mountaineers, climbed in studded shoes over the Grimsel and the

Furka, stopped at Altdorf, crossed the Surenen, and then stayed at Engelberg and Lucerne. After delays on their journey, Felix arrived at Lausanne too late to hear a performance of his *Lobgesang* played at a large concert given by the Swiss Society of Music. But on the following day he was present at a second concert and later at a magnificent ball given in the Grenette, newly decorated for the occasion. The Musée du Vieux-Lausanne retains a lithographed vocal score of the *Lobgesang*.

Once more the happy abundance of his life reclaimed the famous composer, who divided his time between Leipzig and Berlin. He was made an honorary doctor of the University of Leipzig and received the decoration 'Mérite de Prusse' along with Liszt, Meyerbeer, and Rossini. Frederick William IV conferred on him the title of Director-General of Music. In November, he wrote: 'On returning from the performance of my fugue at Dresden, I found Cécile well and in gay high spirits. I can only be grateful for our lot in this world. Our children are splendid'.

A sad event marked the end of the year 1842; the death of Mendelssohn's mother. This remarkable woman had exerted over her family a sort of gentle magnetism. 'When I wrote to my mother, it was to all of you I was writing'. Felix plunged himself into work and experienced again in his private sorrow the wonderfully beneficent influence of Cécile.

February 1843; Berlioz was in Leipzig at the same time as the Hensels. The behaviour of Berlioz somewhat surprised the public, but Felix, as intermediary, restored peace. No doubt the two composers drank together a few of the twenty-four bottles of champagne which the widow Cliquot—whether out of admiration or as a piece of intelligent publicity—never failed to send Felix each year. In parting, Berlioz offered to exchange conductor's batons as a token of friendship. Felix received an enormous stick in exchange for his slender baton covered with white skin. Two months later, in April, Gounod visited Berlin, spending whole days at Fanny Hensel's house discussing music, finally allowing himself to be convinced that his oratorio would be successful in France; after which he began work on *Judith*.

Mendelssohn had long cherised the idea of founding a Conservatoire in Leipzig. At his request, Frederick Augustus II, King of Saxony, put at his disposal a legacy bequeathed to the Crown for the benefit of some artistic institution. So this brilliant German school of music came into being; founded by Mendelssohn, it opened on the 3rd of April, 1843, and had from the outset a large number of pupils. 'This institution', wrote Paul de Stoecklin, 'the crowning achievement of Mendelssohn's life and the object of all his solicitude, was to have a profound and fruitful influence on musical Germany'.

While Mendelssohn was occupied with his public activity and the royal command of Frederick William IV took him once again to Berlin and Potsdam, the domestic life of his family continued harmoniously. Cécile bore a third son—their fourth child—on the 1st of May, 1843, and he was named Felix. 'I am delighted with my three boys', she wrote the following winter. 'Little Felix has already grown into a charming baby. I am told he resembles me, but he frets a little with me and prefers his nurse. I appoint you, my dear Charles, as my agent at the Fahrthor. There are some larks that I have been unable to send grandmother. Julie and I discovered that a peasant woman had some. We immediately bought them and have just sent them

Joseph Joachim.
Drawing by Hermann Grim.
Universal-Edition, Vienna.

Family group at Soden in 1844.

Pencil sketch by Felix Mendelssohn Bartholdy, from the album in the possession of the
Benecke Family, Eastbourne.

off. They will arrive on Friday. Felix left on Monday for Berlin,
where our nephew has just died of measles. Julie Schunck, who
is most pleasant and likable, is staying with me. Your godson
Carl is in splendid health. He came back the other day with his
little bit of nose all red. Seeing the snow he called out "Ooh! Ooh!"
Did you hear that Felix has become deaf and decrepit? The
encyclopaedias, I am told, have known all about it for a long
time. "Se non è vero, è mal trovato!" I write to him every day
in Berlin; give my best wishes to everybody'.

What the king of Prussia particularly wanted at that time
were musical renderings of classical works. Mendelssohn composed *Antigone* and *Athaliah* and produced them at the new
palace in Potsdam. There too he conducted *A Midsummer Night's
Dream*, the incomparable masterpiece which has all the winged
grace of Shakespeare's dream; a work in which, despite his first
misgivings, Mendelssohn's contact with the court finally proved
itself fruitful. A complete score was added, after fifteen years, to
the Overture.

In October, Fanny wrote to her sister:

'Last week the artists from Leipzig arrived here, so as to be
present at the performance; Hiller, David, Gade, and a charming
little Hungarian lad of twelve, Joachim, who plays the violin
so well that David declares he has nothing more to teach the boy.
The first performance of *A Midsummer Night's Dream*, a very
brilliant one, was a perfect success. The public called frantically
for the composer. Felix did not consent to appear'. Thus was
Mendelssohn's prodigious fame spread throughout Germany by
the very work, written in his youth, which had first brought him
celebrity. Mendelssohn's music was inspired by Shakespeare's
poem; together they form two of the major glories of protestant art.

The 'Mendelssohn Bartholdy Sundays', too, were a considerable success at the Dom in Berlin, where *Israel in Egypt*
and other pieces were performed. Felix, against his will, had
reconciled himself to the now famous Berlin, which only a short
while before had been a commonplace city of colonels, generals,

and barracks, a commercial centre with a court that had shown no distinction since the reign of Frederick II. An awakened capital, becoming conscious of musical art under Mendelssohn's influence, Berlin began to pride itself on his brilliant public and private performances. Fanny wrote in March, 1844:

'We have just had the most beautiful of musical Sundays, both as regards the playing and the audience. There were twenty-two carriages in the courtyard; in the hall sat Liszt and eight princesses. As for the programme, there was a quintet by Hummel, followed by a duet from *Fidelio* and variations by David, the last played by that little marvel, Joachim, who is not an infant prodigy, but a wonderful child. Finally, the *Walpurgisnacht.*' In addition, during the winter 1843—44, Mendelssohn had conducted a triumphant and enthusiastic season in London.

After so much effort, Felix spent the summer in well-deserved rest and relaxation. With Cécile and their children, he went for a few months to Soden, in the heart of the German countryside. He took with him only a few blank music sheets and his drawing albums. No more formal dress, visiting-cards, horses and carriages, and no more piano; instead, they wandered about among the flowering fields. They stretched themselves out beneath the trees and sought to find the sky through the foliage. Cécile, too, recovered her energy, and the children, as sunburned and brown as young Arabs, delighted themselves in playing with some small and capricious donkeys. They had to be watched and held by the hand as they rode them in turn through the fields. An unpublished drawing by Felix, recently discovered in England and dated Soden, the 17th of September, 1844, shows the family as it was in the country. Cécile, resting on her elbows, has a book in her hand. The composer's children seem to be chattering and looking at pictures. A table, still covered with the remains of tea, displays a monumental pile of biscuits and cakes.

From Soden, in addition to the letters to Klingemann which have already been published, Felix wrote to Charles Jeanrenaud in Frankfurt. Were they, he asked, really going to play Cherubini's *Medée* at the theatre? Where were certain miniatures of Brentano? Was there a flat vacant for him in Frankfurt, *zum roten Mänche*, where Hiller lived, next to the Souchay's Fahr-

Hall of the old Gewandhaus, Leipzig, in the second half of the nineteenth century.
Photograph kindly lent by History Museum, Leipzig.
After a water colour by Gottlob Theuerkauf.

thor? The famous composer, to whom contentment was a first necessity, nursed continually and in vain the idea of devoting his entire energies to composition. The light whirlwind of his life was to carry him away once more. His plan of returning to a *pied-à-terre* in Frankfurt, while still retaining his residence in Leipzig, was to be realised only temporarily in October, 1844.

Nevertheless, while at Soden, he was able to secure from the Benecke family an old flat *zum roten Mänche* in the same building as his mother-in-law's. Everything was provided for, the distribution of the rooms, the arrangement of the four-poster beds ... The arrival of an array of brushes and brooms was preceded by a consignment of roasted coffee, sugar, butter, and milk: 'Perhaps you can recommend me a milkman; the one who serves the Fahrthor is no good at all', wrote Cécile, living for a time next door to the house in which she was brought up. Amidst these domestic preoccupations of the year 1844, Mendelssohn completed one of his masterpieces, the remarkable Concerto for Violin and Orchestra, dazzling in its power and grace, a rare pearl of intellect and feeling.

One of the major attractions of the concerts at the Gewandhaus in 1845 was the famous cantatrice, Jenny Lind, Mendelssohn's intimate friend and frequently the interpreter of his work. The recipient of honours from the kings and princes of the day, it was she who sang the great song from the *Freischütz*, the first finale in *Euryanthe*, the 'Dove sono' in the *Marriage of Figaro* and a number of *Lieder* which the composer himself accompanied. To give further scope to her talent, he began composing *Loreley*; but this opera, so full of noble promise, was never completed, owing to Mendelssohn's premature death.

The year 1845 saw also the birth, in Leipzig, of Mendelssohn's fifth and last child. This was his second daughter, Lili, born in the autumn. The years of his marriage and the birth of his children, had about them a pastoral and poetic rhythm, and his charming children were born, like rare flowers, into an exquisite landscape of symphonies, concertos, oratorios, psalms, and serenades.

Felix was now thirty-six. He continued to compose, and at the same time he directed the Gewandhaus and the Conservatoire. Two great works of his appeared in 1846. His *Lauda Sion* was first played at Liège, and *Elijah*, the oratorio on which he had been working for ten years, had a triumphant success when it had its first performance in Birmingham on August 26th. It was played in London in the spring of 1847. Mendelssohn arrived on the 12th of April with the young Hungarian,

Joachim. The queen asked him to conduct the performance at Exeter Hall in person. His masterpiece was received with extraordinary applause, and Her Majesty was visibly moved. Prince Albert's enthusiasm was such that he wrote a message of

Watercolour by Felix Mendelssohn, Thun in 1847.
The property of the Wach family, Wilderswil.

homage on his programme and sent it to the composer. The message described Mendelssohn as a noble artist, a prophet who, among those who served Baal, revealed by his transcendent genius, like a new Elijah, the worship of the true God ... *Elijah* was also played in Manchester and Birmingham, where it aroused equal admiration.

Cécile shared in these triumphs. She was present at the performance in London and later in Manchester, where she was

welcomed by the Souchays and the Beneckes. With the true
distinction which became her so well, she occupied a place of
unobtrusive modesty. She herself had a family duty to fulfil
when, at Christmas 1846, she consoled her brother in the misfortune which had recently
befallen them:

'The more we respect
those who went before us, the
more we must seek to re-
semble them and to emulate
their virtues. Think of the
early days of our beloved
grandfather and of his fine
life, beset with difficulties
which he always resolutely
overcame. Did he not bear the
inevitable with gentleness
and patience? If contentment
of mind and peace of soul are
natural gifts, they can none
the less be acquired by effort.
If you desire it, you will attain his serenity. Have confidence in time, which will
bring good, and forgive this
sermon from your ever-loving
Cécile.'

Last portrait of Mendelssohn Bartholdy,
in Switzerland 1847.

From a photograph in the possession of
M. Robert Bory, Coppet.

The 17th of May, 1847,
was one of those grim days
which not even a man singled out for the happiest destiny
can escape. Fanny Hensel, seated at the piano during one of
the famous 'Mendelssohn Sundays', was suddenly seized by
a fainting fit from which she never recovered. She died in Berlin of cerebral extravasation at the age of 42. Felix wrote from
Frankfurt:

Watercolour by Felix Mendelssohn, Interlaken in 1847.
The property of the Wach family, Wilderswil.

'I am overwhelmed with grief and I do not feel I have the courage to leave my wife and children to come and see you, since I can bring you neither help nor consolation. I ought to write otherwise, but I cannot. What can one do, alas! except

Felix Mendelssohn Bartholdy on his death bed.
Drawing by Julius Hubner, the property of the Mendelssohn Bartholdy family.

ask God to grant us a new spirit and a pure heart, so that we may be worthy of her, who had the most upright of minds and an ideal heart! May God bless us and show us His way.'

For Felix, the blow was a heavy one. He had lost a friend who understood him, a companion of his earliest youth: Fanny Hensel, composer in her own right, was no more. Cécile, ever helpful and consolatory, suggested travel; with Hensel, Paul Mendelssohn-Bartholdy, and the children, they set out for

Switzerland, a country which remained for them eternally romantic, a gentle paradise.

After a halt at Baden-Baden, the party entered Switzerland in June via Schaffhausen. They stayed a fortnight at Thun, at the Hotel Bellevue, and then stopped at Interlaken, where they dozed the warm afternoons away in the garden of the Hôtel du Nord. After a holiday of four weeks, Hensel and Paul Mendelssohn-Bartholdy returned to Germany, the one to his painting, the other to his bank. Felix experienced a curious depression, which he had difficulty in overcoming. Arm-in-arm with Cécile, that very part of his being, his supreme consolation and the mainspring of his life, he took long walks in the surrounding country. Little by little his spirits revived. With two of his children, he rode on horseback to Brunig, and in a burst of activity filled his album with luminous watercolour paintings. He felt the necessity of recording in line and colour a landscape which not only impinged on his sight, but permeated his entire being. And having satisfied this need, he began to compose once again. At Interlaken he wrote his Quartet in F minor, a work full of the immense sadness which he felt at the loss of his beloved sister. After travelling through the country round Berne and Neuchâtel, the smiling land which was the home of the Jeanrenauds, Felix and Cécile took the road back to Germany; but not before climbing up to the house at l'Evole which looked out over the blue lake. There Cécile had spent gay holidays as a child, and her old godmother, with tears in her eyes, awaited them.

They drove along the lakeside in a carriage hired in the town, making a sort of pilgrimage to the minister's house at Saint-Aubin, where Alphonse Petitpierre lived; the cousin for whom, ten years before, Cécile had carefully copied out the text of their marriage sermon. Then, via Berne and Basle, in picturesque stages, Felix and his family returned by coach to the green fields of Germany.

Back once more in Leipzig, Mendelssohn suffered a new and mysterious attack, which in spite of all his efforts he had difficulty in overcoming. He did not feel well enough to carry on as director of the Gewandhaus and to conduct the performance of *Elijah* in Berlin. But he had not entirely given up his public offices; it was under his presidency that the examinations for the Conservatoire were held. No one could have expected his premature death.

On the 9th of October he experienced terrible pains in the head, and a few days later he returned from a walk completely exhausted. There is a brief note, dated October the 31st, from Cécile in Leipzig to Mme Dirichlet in Berlin:

'His condition has remained the same for fifteen days. To-day he was once again bled with cupping-glasses. He is feeling better. The doctors assure me that his condition is not dangerous. At the last alarm I sent for Dr. Aarns, who ordered no change in the treatment and is not worried about his progress. I am trying to do the impossible and keep up my spirits, but sometimes it is too difficult ... As I have said, there is for the moment nothing to fear. He needs time ... I shall write again to-morrow.'

A relapse and another cerebral haemorrhage occurred on the 3rd of November. On the following day, only six months after the death of Fanny, he died unconscious in the arms of Cécile and his brother Paul. Undoubtedly the loss of his beloved sister had affected Mendelssohn greatly; nevertheless, his sudden death, in his thirty-ninth year, was a simple and fateful blow falling at the destined hour.

The man who had said: 'My work is a supreme pleasure', was buried in Berlin in the family tomb.

Cécile Mendelssohn Bartholdy.
Drawing by W. Hensel,
the property of M. Paul Léo, Osnabrück.

IX

SOLITUDE

When Ferdinand Hiller arrived in Leipzig, a week after the composer's death, Cécile received him with eyes full of tears, but otherwise showing an admirable restraint, though sorrow had indelibly marked itself on her noble and beautiful face. Hiller had been one of those of whom Felix had often spoken during his illness, and he had been pleased at Hiller's appointment in Düsseldorf.

A great concert of Mendelssohn's works was given in his memory at the Gewandhaus.

Cécile wrote to Jeanne Jeanrenaud: 'Oh God! There is nothing else I can say about this terrible misfortune. I must accept it with patience and resignation. Every day, on waking up, I thank God that I am still well. I was deeply moved by Charles's visit; for several days he helped me to sustain and fortify myself. May heaven preserve your dear family from such sorrows.'

Writing about the terrible misfortune which had parted her daughter from the husband to whom she had devoted the ten finest years of her life, Mme Jeanrenaud noted in her diary: 'With wonderful submissiveness she has bowed to the almighty will. There is in her a greatness worthy of the ancients.'

Mme Dirichlet wrote from Berlin to console her sister-in-law: 'May all the angels help you and preserve you'. In a letter full of anguish and tenderness, she informed Cécile that the whole family were going to the Singakademie, where on the 22nd of November a requiem was to be sung in honour of Felix.

Cécile thanked Queen Victoria: 'Your Majesty has graciously expressed her keen sympathy in the tragic loss which has just been inflicted upon me. If anything could console me for the cruel sorrow which I have just experienced, it would be the affection shown to me from all quarters, and by Your Majesty and His Royal Highness, Prince Albert.

'Unhappily, in such a trial, there is no human consolation. Thanks to the infinite mercy of God, I shall follow alone a path bare of all joy.

In expressing to Your Majesty and to His Royal Highness, Prince Albert, my profoundest gratitude for this kind sympathy, I remain, your very humble,

Cécile Mendelssohn Bartholdy.'

Homage and condolences continued to arrive from all quarters. The famous cantatrice, Jenny Lind—so often closely associated with Mendelssohn Bartholdy in the great concerts, both in Germany and England, at which he had enabled her to make her début in serious music—was shocked by the death of her dearest friend. Wilkens wrote of her: 'The death of Mendelssohn was the first great sorrow in the life of Jenny Lind, and she suffered deeply on account of it. For months, she could not write a letter in which she had to mention the name of Mendelssohn. Everything seemed dead; for a long time she found it impossible to sing any of his lieder. She wrote to his widow:

"You should be very grateful to think how much you were loved and worshipped by someone who was not merely exceptionally gifted, but noble and great! And moreover, yours is the happiness of knowing that he found in you all he had ever sought; through your love and devotion he was borne on the wings of harmony above the whirlwind of an artist's life.

"Could we but meet again in this world, a few words would be sufficient to enable us to understand each other. But one day, we shall all three be together again, and then we shall be happy for ever."'

In a deferential letter from Paris, M. de Tremont, who lived in the Chaussée d'Antin, wrote to Cécile about a manuscript:

'On the 11th of August, 1843, M. Mendelssohn, whom I had the honour of knowing in Paris, was kind enough to compose for me and to send me a "Caprice" for two violins, alto and bass, consisting of an "andante con moto" in E minor, in 12-8 time, followed by an "allegro fugato assai vivace" in C time and in the same key.

'As the manuscript of the score is in my possession, I should be glad to know whether M. Mendelssohn gave a copy for publication to a Leipzig or Berlin publisher. If he did not do so, I could sell this unpublished piece here for the best price obtainable and pay the proceeds of the sale as a contribution to the monument which it is planned to raise to M. Mendelssohn.

'In such a case, would you be kind enough, Madame, to inform me of the town in which this monument is to be erected and of the person in charge of its erection to whom I should transmit this sum of money?

'I hope, Madame, that the motive for my letter will lead you to excuse my presumption in writing.

'I remain, Your very humble and obedient servant,

Baron de Tremont.'

Cécile replied:

'In thanking you for the letter which you were good enough to write, and for the kind intentions which led you to do so, I must point out that for the moment I am unable to accept your offer.

'Neither you nor I have the right to dispose of the score in your possession, the unpublished piece beginning ... and finishing in this time ... The posthumous publication of my husband's works has been postponed until such time as the manuscripts have been re-read and examined by musicians who will be able to decide better than I what is worthy of standing beside the works that my late husband published during his lifetime. That time has not yet been fixed, and for the moment my hands are tied by the judicial settlement of the inheritance.'

Carl Mendelssohn Bartholdy,
eldest son of the composer.
The property of the Mendelssohn Bartholdy
family.

Of the 121 pieces comprising his total work, Mendelssohn, during his lifetime, had published only 73. The remainder did not figure in the catalogues until the time of their publication. The firm of Breitkopf and Härtel, in Leipzig, later published what they claimed to be the complete works of Mendelssohn. But certain fragments have remained unpublished to this day. There are works in the possession of the composer's family which have never been played. As we shall see, Cécile had often to deal with publishers, whose offers lay in wait for her like ambushes. She moved with perfect understanding through this labyrinth of special knowledge.

Having moved with her five children to Berlin, she sometimes needed all her prodigious moral resources to overcome fits of depression during periods when she suffered from a sort of anaemia.

Yet with friends and relatives, she showed always the touching, romantic sensitivity which was characteristic of her. In writ-

ing to her brother-in-law, Paul Mendelssohn-Bartholdy, she herself painted marigolds and bell-flowers on the sheet of paper which she had delivered to him by hand:

'Since I am tied down, a sort of prisoner in a suit of armour, and I am unable to get up and visit you, here are my fingertips.' In another letter she confides in him: 'I have a deep sense of compassion for Hensel, and although our ways of thinking often differ, we are bound by our common feeling of being opposed by a cruel fate. Droysen highly recommends for Carl

Paul Mendelssohn Bartholdy,
second son of the composer.
The property of the Mendelssohn Bartholdy
family.

the "gymnasium" of which Professor Ranke is the principal. Would you find out from Ganz and Ries about a violin master for Paul? Someone with patience, from the orchestra. Marie is making great progress with the piano.'

Droysen, Ranke, Ganz, and Hubert Ries were all men of

note. The last, a former pupil at the violin school of Spohr, had become royal concert-master in Berlin. He was a well-known teacher and later published a standard work entitled, "Violin Method". Cécile's circle remained a distinguished one.

On the 3rd of January, 1848, Felix's birthday, flowers arrived from all quarters. They filled the house with their perfume, and Cécile was moved to tears at the sympathy expressed by these gifts. She wrote to her brother-in-law:

'Except for myself, no one, my dear Paul, loved Felix as deeply as you. May you continue to feel a similar affection towards me; that will help me to carry on. My past happiness seems to me to have become a sort of thick veil which obscures the future. Come what may, future years can never deprive me of the fantastic enchantment of having belonged to Felix. Short as our life together was, it was filled with a pure and indescribable happiness. Every day I become more unsociable; I have to be forced to go out. I do not want to re-read Felix's letters too often. Have you already examined the files of correspondence which he had bound? I am thinking of going soon to visit my uncle and aunt at Ems and Horchheim. Please give my loving regards to Albertine and the children.'

In May of this year, 1848, Albertine gave birth to a son, Gotthold Mendelssohn-Bartholdy, who later married a daughter of the Wentz family. He and his brother, Ernest von Mendelssohn-Bartholdy, finally became the heads of the Mendelssohn-Bartholdy family (spelt with the hyphen) which was descended from Paul, the composer's brother. 'I was delighted to hear the expected news of Albertine's confinement. How happy you must be, my dear Paul! I refuse to believe that the baby was born—too soon!' A short while afterwards, a note from Cécile reveals that the Berliners were using somewhat drastic methods to obtain milk in the Leipzigerstrasse itself ... 'Do you still keep your magnificent cow? I am sending you some boxes of letters and manuscripts of great importance for the future; please take care of them. You have no idea how meticulous and conscientious Felix

was. I shall always look upon the preservation of his correspondence as a great responsibility. The letters belonging to the period
after 1837 I could go through myself, as I am probably better
informed about them than you. Don't you think that the
Härtels will go ahead with the publication of a complete bio-
graphy? Wouldn't it be better for you to keep your project
separate from Frank's?' She is referring to the documents and
the famous correspondence which, when published later, revealed,
to the public's surprise, that Felix was a writer, as well as a
composer.

In supervising the education of her children, Cécile showed
herself capable and far-seeing, following their development step
by step. She and the children were occupying, for the time being,
a fine ground-floor flat in the Prussian capital, at 22 Jägerstrasse. Opposite the windows of the flat grew a walnut-tree,
which was always being shaken by climbing boys, and so afforded
the children an abundant harvest. This was in September.

Among other matters mentioned in the numerous letters,
dated 1848, which Cécile wrote to her relatives, she refers to the
financial provision for the children's future. 'This morning I
signed, together with Paul, a document which had already been
drawn up in Leipzig at the suggestion of Schleinitz. In it I assure
the children's rights of inheritance according to Saxon law,
although the whole matter must be finally settled here. How
slow they are.'

Various trustees were appointed for the children in an effort
to clarify a situation in which many interests were inextricably
mixed, and which was complicated by author's rights and agree-
ments planned or actually in force. If Cécile was capable of
handling musical matters, she confessed to understanding little
where figures were concerned. 'You know', she said to Paul,
'how good and tolerant Felix was, although he might well have
been disturbed by one of my faults. He told me again last year:
"We shall never learn, my dear, to talk reasonably together
about business matters . . ." I thought, without reflecting

properly, that since our property was in your hands, things would carry on in the same way as when he was alive. I did not suspect that, so long as the complicated inheritance of Felix's fortune had not yet come into force, I should be dependent on you. Being unaware of that, I had refused an offer from my uncle Souchay, who is administering the fortune invested in our business in England, which will in due course pass to my mother. Shall I have to draw up a monthly budget? Let me know, please.'

Paul Mendelssohn-Bartholdy, as well as being an excellent 'cellist, was a highly competent banker. Both his professional experience and his musical knowledge were needed to unravel the tangle of an inheritance in which property and furniture were mixed up with operas, hymns, anthems, songs, and symphonies ... Had it been only a question of classifying works furnished with their text for publication, the situation would perhaps have been less delicate. However, some twenty letters from Cécile to Paul show that she was able to master not only the general difficulties of publication, but also the more specialised questions of literary adaptation. Her own judgement was excellent, but she did not hesitate to seek advice:

'Dear Paul, Mr. Buxton writes that when he spoke to Felix about *Lauda Sion*, Felix wanted him to ask M. Bartholomé for a protestant text, or a text adapted to the music in such a way that the work could be published in Latin and in English. M. Bartholomé therefore wrote such a text. Felix was not opposed to a protestant text which would be translated into English. However, since the work was composed in the first instance for the catholic text, we ought to keep to the Latin text. Mr. Buxton says that the English text has been adapted well, except for one passage which will have to be changed. Felix gave no opinion about a German text. Do you think that, although he authorised a protestant text in England, he would have permitted a German text? I recollect that he insisted on the *catholic* character of *Lauda Sion*. He used that expression several times. Dr. Härtel has also written to me about the text of *Athaliah* ...'

'I am writing to you from Frankfurt, where I am just on the point of taking the coach. I am enclosing with these few lines an album for Hensel and figures for printing on fabric which were given to Felix by some good friends of his; you will shortly be receiving his desk. Please accept it from me. He too dedicated it to you; on it he wrote his last lines. I part from it with regret, but to you I give it willingly. The Schleinitz have the chest containing Felix's manuscripts. Rietz and Schleinitz still have to discuss them; it is a question of making an exact inventory of his themes. If you wish to have these pieces, ask Schleinitz for them. I should not like them to travel alone . . .

'The question of the "marches" has been settled. Klingemann has offered to compose the German text of *Lauda Sion*. It will not be a translation, but a protestant, biblical text. What do you think about it? Are you opposed to having the music of *Athaliah* printed soon? Rietz made the score for the piano and played it to me. I took a great pleasure in hearing it. Mme Frege, who knows the score by heart, was present. Everyone would have been sorry to see this work neglected. As I promised, I asked Härtel to give the money for the piano score to Rietz, who would not have accepted it from me. Have you any objection to the publication of this score for the piano?'

Jules Rietz, mentioned in Cécile's letter, was the well-known master who took over the direction of the Gewandhaus on Felix's death. He had studied the 'cello from an early age with Romberg and Ganz, and had already succeeded Mendelssohn in Düsseldorf. A composer of renown, he wrote overtures, operas, symphonies, and miscellaneous pieces, and continued the movement begun by Felix for the popularisation of the work of Bach. He also assisted in the publication of work by Mozart and Beethoven.

Further extracts from letters to Paul:

'I am sending you the English translation of the text of *Lauda Sion*. My very modest acquaintance with English literary style does not permit me to judge its worth. In Leipzig,

Monicke told me that the adaptation had been done well. I thought that a less literal text would better have served Felix's public in England. If Klingemann intervenes, matters will drag on for some time. Because of the Revolution, I have been unable to make contact with Schott, in Mainz, where the work was to have been printed in accordance with a contract signed by Felix. Dr. Härtel asked me to agree, for publication purposes, to his buying back from Schott and Kistner all that Felix left in their hands. I first of all refused, suspecting a piece of business speculation on their part. But as regards the other works, I felt that it would be preferable to deal with the Härtels, who are more adaptable than other publishers. Advise me, in case they should approach me again.

'Don't you think that Geibel should be asked to compose the poetic text adapted to the music of *Athaliah* before some niggling poet meddles with it?'

On another occasion, Cécile wrote to her brother-in-law:

'Many thanks for sending me the inventory of Felix's property. I do not in the least understand it, except for the last part. The extraordinary claims of the publishers have in no way diminished. Recently the conductor of the Coblenz orchestra wrote to say that he has in his possession copies of certain scores of church music written by Felix, which were sent to him for performance by the Prussian minister. He thinks that these scores are the personal property of the king, and wants to ask him for permission to publish them. He proposes to use the money for the foundation of a Mendelssohn fund. He asks if I have any objection. I have many objections; no doubt you have, too? I was in any case unaware that Felix had surrendered his author's rights over works written for the special pleasure of His Majesty. I think that this conductor in Coblenz should be politely forbidden to publish. It appears from the tone of his letter that he would submit to such a decision. A singularly clumsy and German way of behaving! I have sent Schleinitz this request from Coblenz, with the list of church choirs which Felix collected, as well as the numbers of works corresponding to the motets which appeared later.

'I intend to leave my mother here, in Leipzig, until the autumn, since we still have the use of the house. Enclosed is a programme sent to me from New York by the president of the Philharmonic Society, of which Felix was a member. It contains an account of the way in which the news of his death was received. Members of the Society wore mourning for thirty days. A great concert, to which admission was free, was given in his memory, and all the musical societies and groups in New York were represented. As you see, they played Beethoven's *Marche Funèbre*, numerous pieces of various kinds from *Saint Paul* and *Elijah*, recitatives, duets, chorales, quartets, *Recordare* of Mozart's requiem, a duet and chorus from the *Lobgesang*, and in conclusion the great chorus from *Saint Paul: Wach auf, du Stadt Jerusalem!* I think that the programme was very well arranged.'

As Cécile's letter shows, it was not only in the towns of Germany, France, and England that the memory of the musical genius of Mendelssohn was honoured. Long before his death, his reputation had spread to America, where his work was widely appreciated, appealing as it did, not only to an artistic minority, but to the vast general public.

Cécile was still quite undecided about where to make her permanent home. 'It is not true to say that I shall always live in Berlin. I consider it a duty to bring the children up there, but I would also wish, if God grants me life, to keep my mother company in the evening of her days.'

There is a moving letter (hitherto unpublished) from Mme Jeanrenaud, Cécile's distinguished mother, to Paul Mendelssohn-Bartholdy. It is dated the 1st of July, 1848:

'The beauty of days gone by lives still in our memory like a picture surrounded by light mist. We all want to honour it, to respect it, as the finest thing in the present bareness of our lives. I am obeying my heart and my conscience alone in speaking to you openly. Cécile's nature has from childhood been gentle, but a little secretive. One always had to guess at more than she actually expressed. Now my dear girl is dazed by the terrible

Madame Auguste Jeanrenaud, née Souchay, in later life,
with her grand daughter, Lili Mendelssohn Bartholdy, afterwards Mme Wach.
Retouched photograph, the property of Dr Felix Wach, Radebeul.

blow which has deprived her of her immense happiness. She can hardly see further than the immediate details of her existence and is not up to the task of estimating and dominating her present circumstances. Her children, or at any rate her sons, seem to feel their ties mainly with their father's family. I realize that as well as Cécile. The love shown to them by dear Felix's brother and sister makes them wish to settle in Berlin. On the other hand, Cécile feels that, after so great a misfortune, nothing in the world can take the place of her childhood surroundings and the beneficent influence of first affections, those of her mother. The happiness of a mother is transmitted to her children, and *vice versa* If my daughter decided to live for a few years with your family, to find once again resignation and gaiety, I should watch her go with pleasure, since she would be received by you with open arms and since, too, that would satisfy the children's wishes. As things are, I can think of her doing so only with sadness. However, Cécile seems to me to be stronger than I should have been in similar circumstances. But she hides her sorrow. Her serenity is on the surface. A deep unhappiness disturbs and torments her. Alas! Believe me, I have learned that only the help of God and the love of those who taught us our first steps, our first words, and whose heart is an open book to us—only these and the soothing hand of passing time can soften so deep and bitter a pain.'

Thus, in her long, gentle, and heartfelt letter, from which only a short passage has been quoted, Mme Jeanrenaud gave it as her disinterested opinion that Cécile—who was quite unaware of her mother's step—would really be able to find herself again only in Frankfurt. She encouraged the holiday journeys which Cécile was planning and enclosed with her own letter two precious confidential letters from Felix, which would no doubt convince his brother. 'May God bless the dear, dear hand which wrote them', she added, 'the hand which is now still, but which seems only to be resting. It is immortal, and in another life it will open once again to welcome a beloved wife, children, a brother, sisters, and all of us, when there will be no more tears and no more separation.'

Numerous friends invited Cécile to visit them, in an attempt to alleviate her distress, while her doctors advised a spa or a change of altitude. But believing that her duty required it, she insisted on continuing to live in Berlin.

Some of her letters at this period are coloured with picturesque details of the household. There was, for instance, the question of a manservant named Franz. To get rid of him, they could not but wish keenly that he should be called up for military service. Meanwhile, the incalculable wave of revolution which had begun in Paris rolled on through the continent.

'Dear Paul', she wrote in a letter (dated the 19th of September, 1848) from Frankfurt, where she was paying a visit, 'the papers will no doubt have given a long account of yesterday's events. On Saturday and on Sunday evening, there were already large mobs in the town. Yesterday troops arrived from Mainz, about two thousand Austrians and Prussians, who occupied the squares and the church of Saint Paul. At midday, there were fights and riots in front of the church. The soldiers intervened and used stalls from the fair as material for raising barricades. There was a lot of firing all through the day, while trains brought up more contingents from Darmstadt and Würtemburg. They say that many people were killed. In the evening, 10 000 men were masters of the town. To-day there is complete calm; all the houses are overflowing with soldiers.' It was to Frankfurt that the German revolutionaries sent delegates for the memorable constituent assembly.

Two months later, Cécile was settled in Berlin, in the house owned by the Mendelssohn Bartholdy family in the Leipziger-strasse. It was melancholy, living once again, but this time without Felix, in the deserted old house belonging to his family. 'My sister-in-law has arranged everything comfortably for me; everything reminds me so vividly of Felix; the lovely garden, silent and sad, is my favourite place.' This large old house had been bought in 1825 in a dilapidated condition from the von der Reck family; after having been restored, it remained in the hands of the Mendelssohn Bartholdys for about twenty-five years. Not long after Cécile's occupation of the house in 1848, it was sold to accomodate the Upper Chamber of Prussia. The magnificent foliage of the immense garden, which formerly adjoined that of Prince Albert, still had the power to produce in Cécile a tender, romantic reverie. But alas! No more princely receptions ... No more of the famous 'Mendelssohn Sundays'...

She was often worried about the health of Felix, her youngest son; and in some of the forty letters which she wrote at this period to Charles and Jeanne Jeanrenaud, her brother and sister, she complained, too, of herself feeling unwell: 'The doctors want me to go somewhere in the mountains; I often feel very poorly. If Charles doesn't think my little Lili pretty, he'll have me to deal with! At this moment she's crying and strikingly resembles him!' Following with love the development of her children, guiding them, supporting them, encouraging them in all circumstances, Cécile was always busy and struggled courage-ously on their behalf. In March 1849, she sang with her friends, Countess Charlotte de Bronilowka and Henriette de Mechel of Basle, in a choir conducted by Julius Stern. In May, she stayed with her relatives in Charlottenburg. She found the newspapers uninteresting: 'I see few people and never read the papers. God has granted that everything should flourish and prosper here as ever'. She hesitates to go and join the Jeanrenauds in Creutz-nach. 'Many families have fled from Leipzig. What a terrible misfortune it was that happened to M. Gonthard! I do not want ever to be separated from my children by the vicissitudes of war. How could they ravage such a beautiful town as Dresden? Did the progress of civilisation have to lead to so shameful a war as this?'

From Schlangenbad, on the green borders of the Taunus, Cécile Mendelssohn Bartholdy wrote two letters on the 21th of August, 1849: one, written to her brother, I discovered ninety years later in Rio de Janeiro; the other, to the famous painter Moscheles, I found in the castle of Miltenberg, on the banks of the Main. Both written on the same day, with the same ink and the same finely shaped pen, these twin manuscripts have been carefully preserved by her relatives and are now lying together on my desk as I write these notes: side by side, they bring to us over the years a sort of warmth, as of Cécile herself, the living presence of that delightful woman, whose simple charm of spirit and greatness of soul more than deserve such modest homage as I am able to render her. These two letters, like so many others, have no pretensions; yet they show us Cécile adapting herself, with spirit and understanding, to the personality of the recipient. To Charles she writes with affection, conveys to him the taste of 'the frightful whey that I have just drunk', describes her bathes with her daughter Marie, and does not forget to perfume her letter with the delicious scents of the forest. To Moscheles she writes mainly a business letter:

Cécile Mendelssohn Bartholdy.
Painted by Jacob Becker.
From a copy belonging to M. Henry de Bary, Frankfurt.

'I was unable to give you any news until I had got in touch with Herr Simrock, the publisher of *Elijah*. As this oratorio appeared six months before my husband's death, I thought that all the negotiations were over. But for your reminder, I should have done no more about it. Herr Simrock replies that M. Lemoine has the rights for France only and that he himself has reserved the right to negotiate with a fellow-publisher, if he should eventually find one, who is in a position to launch the work. The German copy has been registered in Paris in accordance with the recognized procedure. Shortly afterwards, Mme Lanner came along with an offer to M. Lemoine of the usual royalties. However, she withdrew her offer when M. Brandus, Schlessinger's successor, informed her that *Elijah* was to be published by him as part of the *domaine public.* Thereupon, Herr Simrock asked M. Lemoine to put the matter in the hands of a lawyer. The revolution put an end to the legal proceedings. Herr Simrock thinks that by restating the case he can persuade M. Brandus to withdraw from the affair.

Charles Jeanrenaud, 1814—1891,
lawyer and member of the Court of Appeal, Frankfurt.
Drawing belonging to Mme de Coulon-Jeanrenaud,
Château de Miltenberg.

I asked him to go ahead quickly with his discussions and I should greatly regret it if, on account of such paltry legal quibbling, a magnificent opportunity of presenting this work in a worthy fashion should be lost. Personally, I can do nothing. The matter is in the hands of the French law. Let us hope that Mme Viardon's wish is realised. Thank you also for your efforts on behalf of this oratorio. Your judgement on recent musical events in London, which were so diversely described in the press, interested me greatly . . . ' As can be seen, the problems of public-ation were not at all easy. In a light vein, Cécile adds a few impulsive lines for Char-lotte, the wife of Moscheles, to whom, apparently, she bore suddenly a strange re-semblance, judging from the sprightly conversation of a lady of her acquaintance, a fellow-bather from Antwerp.

Jeanne Jeanrenaud, née de Bihl.
(From a photograph).

In Berlin, at the end of October, after congratulating herself on the fact that the cholera epidemic had spared her children, she was driven by the indescribable din they made playing in the house, to recall her great love of *silence*: 'Now that winter is here, I must very soon get myself a new pair of ears'. Apart from Carl, the eldest, who was slow in developing, her chil-dren received splendid re-ports from their schools in Berlin. Their studies were super-vised, too, by M. Groos, their tutor.

Holidays at Kreutznach and Schlangenbad broke the long summers of 1850 and 1851. In the autumn, they returned once again to Berlin: 'Tell mother not to worry; I am pleased with the children and I suffer less from loneliness. I had all Felix's relatives to dinner; there were nineteen of us. We take it in turn to lunch at each other's houses on Sundays. A gentleman has sent me four smoke-cured geese from Pomerania.'

These were slender consolations for the heavy blows of fate which were shortly to shatter her life once more. The death of her son Felix was a terrible ordeal. All her thoughts centred round that fragile and brief existence. She worshipped the two sons and two daughters who remained to her, yet she could not but look at the future with dismay, and with a feeling of darkness and defeat. Her health was affected. All she could do was to maintain her unalterable personal code of behaviour; to continue uprightly to do her duty. Yet another death occurred in the family. Mme Jeanrenaud lost her mother, Hélène Souchay, who died in the Fahrthor in 1851, after having been widowed several years before. It was at this time, while Cécile was paying a visit to Frankfurt, that Jacob Becker[1] asked her to sit for her portrait.

Flowers painted at Vevey by Cécile Mendelssohn.
Property of the Wach family, Wilderswil.

Charles Jeanrenaud de Bihl was living in a small house which had long been in the possession of the de Bihl family and which was tucked away in a corner of one of the Schaumainkai gardens

---

[1] Jacob Becker, born in 1810, near Worms, was first of all a lithographer. In 1833, studying with Schirmer, he began to paint landscapes. After a further period of study in Düsseldorf, he became a teacher of art and history in Frankfurt. In his work, which was romantic in character, he made a wonderful use of colour. From 1842 onwards, he painted very many portraits of well-known people, including that of Cécile Mendelssohn Bartholdy; also, numerous landscapes and scenes of country life. His best known paintings are 'Der Ritter und sein Liebchen', 'Die betende Bauernfamilie', and 'Der heimkehrende Krieger'. He will long be remembered for his association with the Stadel Institute in Frankfurt.

in Frankfurt. His letters were full of a plan to build a fine house for the Jeanrenauds in this same garden; Cécile, from Berlin, commented so expertly on the plans sent to her that one might have thought her an architect. She insisted that some larches should not be cut down, as they interfered neither with the view

Approaching Chillon.
Painting in oils by Cécile Mendelssohn, the property of the Wach family, Wilderswil.

nor with the light; the shadow of these fine trees would stretch out over the lawn behind a pretty ironwork fence and over the roads leading up to the projected house. Erected in 1852, the house was later well known in Frankfurt as the 'Jeanrenaud House'. Its site was then still almost in open country, on the south bank of the Main, from which the Fahrthor of the Souchays could be seen upstream, on the other side of the river and in line with the north quay.

For Mme Jeanrenaud, at the age of 55, the emptiness of the Fahrthor, with its memories of so many of the departed, became cruelly painful. Memories and disappointments called for a change of scene; a journey through beautiful surroundings could provide

Painting in oils by Cécile Mendelssohn Bartholdy
'By the Italian lakes'
The property of the Wach family, Wilderswil

its traditional consolation. Such was Cécile's suggestion to her
mother, who was experiencing a mood of overwhelming grief,
in which she clung devotedly to her faith in the French Church.
'I suggest *la Suisse française*, particularly as we have so many
relatives and friends there. I myself would very much like to

Near Assisi
Painting in oils by Cécile Mendelssohn Bartholdy
The property of the Wach family, Wilderswil

go with her, but I cannot say now whether I could get away.
Mother has very pleasant memories of Switzerland. We recently
went with her to Pastor André, who had invited many people
from Neuchâtel to his house. How pleased she was to meet
people from her part of the country who had known our father
well. And how pleased, too, to hear accounts of La Chaux-de-
Fonds and the Locle.'

Mme Jeanrenaud, her daughter Julie, Cécile, and the children, after their holiday by the Italian lakes—where Cécile
had begun to paint again—soon paid their projected visit

to *la Suisse française*. They made contact once again with all
their relatives, and then stayed at Vevey, where M. Monnet
spoiled them with his hospitality. The snowy cascade of the
Giessbach aroused the children's delight; the melancholy of the
Neuchâtel shores captured their hearts; and the supreme beauty
of the Lake of Geneva filled them all with admiration. Their
absence from Germany was prolonged. Christmas 1851 and the
New Year saw the exchange of presents between Vevey, Neuchâtel, Saint Aubin, La Chaux-de-Fonds, and Berlin. On the
10th of May, 1852, shortly before leaving the shores of the Lake
of Geneva, Cécile sent a cordial message to her cousin Cornelia
Schunck, in Priesnitz:

'On my balcony, beside this exquisite lake which you know
so well, I often think of you as I look out towards the Alps of
Savoy or into the *fond du lac* as the people here say. With
what emotion do I watch the ever-changing gleam of lake and
mountains, those precious, silent friends of mine. Before returning to Berlin, we shall stop at Geneva, and afterwards in the
Alps.' They were in fact still travelling in Italy at the time this
letter was written.

In the year 1852 Cécile lost further relatives. 'I feel an
immense grief', she wrote from Berlin, 'at the news of the death
of Aunt Charlotte Petitpierre, who was so kind and good; she
had a great affection for me, and as my godmother she inspired
in me both love and respect. I shall always remember with
pleasure our last visit to Neuchâtel, when she extended a most
agreeable welcome to us in her charming house. I shall remember,
too, the pride with which she showed us her plants and the view
over the lake, which struck me every time I stepped out of the
house. The news of her death has moved me deeply, amid my own
unhappy memories. As it is, I find it very difficult to get through
my daily life'. These lines were written in November, the same
month in which, five years before, she had lost her ideal partner.

In spite of the state of her health, which seemed to have
worsened even on the Riviera-like shores of the Lake of Geneva,

Cécile Mendelssohn Bartholdy tried to resume with courage and calm her round of duty. Hiller speaks of a visit he paid to her house. 'My visit was a profoundly moving experience. The pleasant and natural chatter of the children, the gentle and charming way in which Cécile tried to moderate their liveliness, left me quite astounded. What joy they could have given to him who is now dead! And what joy he could have given them!'

The manuscript of the last letter written by Cécile Mendelssohn Bartholdy is lying before me; it is addressed to Neuchâtel from Berlin and is dated the 10th of January, 1853. At the beginning of this year whose end she was not to see, Cécile wrote once again, this time from her sick-bed, to Julie Petitpierre, her father's god-daughter. In four long pages, she refers to the death of her godmother, and, seeking as always to surround her thoughts with an evocative picture, she brings to life the interiors of rooms and the flowered terraces of that corner of the Neuchâtel country which she loved so well. Then she adds:

'Formerly I lived here, too, amid sweet memories; I enjoyed them. How I loved my mother-in-law's old house, with its large courtyard and its immense, dark garden, whose every bush reminded me of the beautiful days now gone. This winter, when I am frequently unwell and feel ill-at-ease in my new house, I often say to myself that we are but travellers in this world, and that in this life there is no homeland.

'My dear Julie, I shall not try to say anything consoling. I know that you and your family seek consolation where it is to be found. Please remember me to Alphonse and his dear wife and kiss the children for me. Also mention me to Aunt Sandoz, Uncle and Aunt Jeanrenaud, and Uncle Wurflein. My children speak a great deal, and with affection, about Switzerland, and I am sure that the memory will remain with them throughout their lives ...'

Some of Mendelssohn's biographers relate that after his death his wife retired to Frankfurt. That was not so. Such was Mme Jeanrenaud's wish, as we have seen, and perhaps Cécile's secret wish too. Nevertheless, she maintained her intention of bringing the children up in Berlin.

The state of her health grew so much worse, during the summer of 1853, that she came to Frankfurt, where her mother surrounded her in the old Fahrthor with attentions born out of a feeling of desperation. It was in this beloved house on the bank of the Main, the house in which she had spent her whole childhood and put on her bridal veil, that Cécile Mendelssohn Bartholdy was to die of a disease of the lungs which stealthily undermined her.

Her aunt, Mme Souchay (née Schmidt), wife of Senator Souchay, describes her death in a letter to her son at Vogelsang, in the Wesel, on the 26th of September, 1853:

'I spent Saturday at the Fahrthor and found Cécile very ill. About six o'clock in the evening, on my way home, I returned to the Fahrthor, where I was immediately told that Cécile was having violent choking fits. I went up to her room and found her in an indescribable state. She took both my hands and said, "Auntie, I beg of you, don't leave me again. I have no one; I don't want my mother to come in, she suffers too much when she sees my condition." I stayed beside her. As soon as I made to go out, she called me back. I sent for Uncle Adolphe (Dr Schmidt) who told me that it was impossible to move her from there, it would be agony for her. Cécile was short of breath. She kept crying: "Air! Air! I am choking!" It was terrible . . .

'At ten o'clock in the evening, she said to me, "Auntie, you didn't get any sleep last night, you must go home." Adolphe thought she might take fright if I stayed after all; but I told her that she would not drive me away, and that I did not want to cross the Main in the storm and the rain. She smiled and said, "I am very glad". Everybody had gone to bed, she seemed a little easier, and Uncle Adolphe wanted her to be left alone; she did not like anyone to see her suffer. She prayed often and liked me to read to her from the Bible. She smiled and pressed my hand.

'At five o'clock in the morning, I went to wake the maid. At seven o'clock, I sent for father, Charles Jeanrenaud, Uncle Adolphe, but Cécile would not let me leave her. She repeated, "I have prayed so much to God to grant me a peaceful end!"

Cécile Mendelssohn Bartholdy on her death bed in 1853.
Retouched drawing by her brother-in-law, W. Hensel.
The property of the Wach family, Wilderswil.

'Her wish was granted. Half-an-hour before dying, she fell asleep, at first breathing peacefully, and then ceasing to breathe so imperceptibly that we did not notice it until a few minutes afterwards. It was one o'clock in the afternoon. A little while later, her brother-in-law, Paul Mendelssohn-Bartholdy arrived from Berlin.

'The night before, at ten o'clock, she had kissed her right hand and held it out to me. Then, as though thinking of Felix, she had raised her eyes upwards for a long time, kissed her hand again, and sent her greeting heavenwards.'

Thus, shortly before her death on the 25th of September, 1853, at the age of thirty-six, Cécile Mendelssohn Bartholdy had greeted with a confident and sublime gesture the Christian husband whom the certainty of her faith told her she was about to find, shining and faithful, in glory.

'It was the 25th of September, 1853', wrote Hiller. 'I made my way to the Fahrthor and tugged at the little bell whose familiar tinkling I had so often heard when, in former days, I had stood there eagerly looking forward to some most delightful hours. Hardly had I been admitted, when Mme Jeanrenaud rushed out of a room and said in a subdued voice, "Ah, it's you, my dear Hiller. I have just this moment lost my daughter", she added, with the terrible calm of despair.'

A last extract from Senator Souchay's diary:

'Cécile, in 1851, had been overwhelmed by the death—after eighteen days of frightful suffering—of her son Felix, whose expressive and serious portrait has been painted by the famous Magnus. Shortly afterwards, there appeared on my poor niece's face a sad foreboding. She did not complain, neither when she took with me a last walk to Heidelberg, nor when her brother and I had suddenly to carry her in pain to her dear room beside the Main. To-day this rare flower has bowed its head; the gentle soul of Cécile has rejoined Felix in eternity.'

X

CONCLUSION

In the old cemetery of Frankfurt, with its lofty portico, among the tombstones rising like motionless and weary harvesters at the end of their labour, stands a rustic cross of Italian marble above the grave of Cécile Mendelssohn Bartholdy. Here, too, are buried other members of the Jeanrenaud family, including Cécile's brother, Dr Charles Jeanrenaud, lawyer and counsellor in the city's Court of Appeal (died 1891), and his wife, Jeanne de Bihl, whose mother, née Textor, was a near relative of Goethe. Nearby are the graves of their two sons, Alexandre-Carl and Carl Auguste Jeanrenaud, who died in 1873 and 1903. To the right of Cécile, her mother is buried; Elisabeth-Wilhelmine Jeanrenaud-Souchay died in 1871 and retained to the end her courage and her spirit. All these tombs, in their green surroundings, resemble each other in their dignity and simplicity. Small gilt lettering sadly recalls the names, dates, and birthplaces of the dead. The cross of precious marble which stands above Cécile's ivycovered grave is a symbol; unadorned grey rock, it brings to mind the modesty and purity of her life.

After her daughter's death, Mme Jeanrenaud had drawn closer to her family in Neuchâtel, where political events and revolution had severed the district's connection with Germany. She lived mainly with her son, in the house which the Jeanrenauds owned in the Schaumainkai. This house, after passing into his children's hands, was later sold; but like the Fahrthor of the Souchays, it still stands (it is No. 43) and before the war, having undergone alterations, it housed the Polish Consulate.

Here, before concluding, are a few genealogical details of

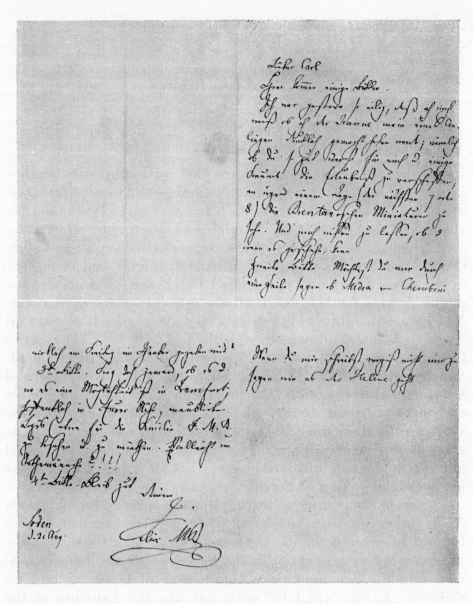

Letter of the 21st of August, 1844, from Felix Mendelssohn to Charles Jeanrenaud.

The property of Mme de Coulon-Jeanrenaud,
Miltenberg Château.

Page from a letter in French written by Cécile Mendelssohn Bartholdy to her cousin Julie Petitpierre in Neuchâtel.

Dated from Berlin, the 10th of January, 1853.

Mendelssohn's descendants, of whom there were a considerable number. The first generation consisted of Felix and Cécile's two sons, Carl and Paul, and two daughters, Marie Benecke[1] and Lili Wach[2].

Neither of the composer's two sons entered the banking house founded by their grandfather. Paul, Felix's brother, had become head of the firm, and he was succeeded in this position by Felix's nephew and grand-nephew.

Carl, elder son of Felix and Cécile, was born in Leipzig in 1838. His education, as well as that of his brother and his sisters, all of them orphaned at an early age, was received in Frankfurt and Berlin, under the care both of the Jeanrenauds and their devoted uncle, Paul Mendelssohn - Bartholdy - Heine. Carl became a distinguished hi-

Marie Benecke, Mendelssohn's daughter

From a photograph

---

[1] *The Benecke family.* In an earlier footnote on the Schunck family, details were given of the descendants of Marie Mendelssohn, Felix's daughter, and her husband, Victor Benecke. This branch of the composer's family is represented by Marie's children, the late Dr Paul Benecke, professor at Oxford University, and his sister, Miss Marguerite Benecke, of Eastbourne. Their brother, Edouard Benecke, was killed on a climbing expedition in the Jungfrau mountains, which Felix had admired so much; Edouard Benecke's body was never recovered.

[2] *The Wach family.* Lili Mendelssohn Bartholdy married Adolphe Wach, already a well-known jurist. The marriage was celebrated in the charming 'Jeanrenaud House' in the Schaumainkai, where Mendelssohn's children had spent part of their childhood. Adolphe Wach was born on the 11th of September, 1843, at Culm, in East Prussia. In 1869, he began teaching law in Rostock, and in 1875 he became a professor in Leipzig. His publications and commentaries on civil and criminal law soon made him the most prominent jurisconsult in Germany. The king of

storian and the author of several works, notably a 'History of Greece from 1453 to the present day'. He was a professor at Heidelberg and Freiburg im Breisgau and died in 1897. He was twice married, on the first occasion to a member of the Eissenhardt family, and on the second to a member of the von Merkl family. By his second wife he had a remarkably gifted son, Dr Albrecht Mendelssohn Bartholdy (married Miss Wach), professor of international law at Hamburg and other German universities, and later at Oxford. He gained for himself a splendid reputation as a director of institutes and reviews of political science and as an expert delegate to arbitration courts and international courts of law. He was a member of the tribunal for the interpretation of the Dawes

His Excellency Dr Adolphe Wach
Famous German jurisconsult
From a photograph

Saxony chose him as his private counsellor and bestowed on him the title of Excellency. Adolphe Wach, posthumous son-in-law of the great composer, died in Leipzig on the 4th of April, 1926, leaving six children, who are still alive and do honour to his memory. They are: Dr and Counsellor Felix Wach, of Radebeul, Professor Hugo Wach, of Berlin, Mme Elisabeth de Steiger, of Basle, Mrs. Albrecht Mendelssohn Bartholdy (née Dora Wach) of Clifton Hampden, Miss Marie Wach, of Wilderswil (who has preserved in 'le Ried', among the tranquil firs facing the Eiger, numerous relics of the Mendelssohn Bartholdy and Jeanrenaud families), and Dr Adolphe Wach, a Zurich lawyer.

Further generations have stemmed from the children of Adolphe and Lili Wach. Among others, Felix Wach's sons have distinguished themselves; one is a professor of religious philosophy in the University of Leipzig, another a minister in the Protestant Church, and others have entered the professions.

Plan and he prepared for publication documents on the origins of the first World War which appeared in 1921 and 1926. He died on the 27th of November, 1936, leaving a widow and two adopted daughters.

Paul, Felix and Cécile's son, was born at Leipzig in 1841, and very soon gave signs of a brilliant talent. Having matriculated, he entered the Faculty of Philosophy of Heidelberg University in 1859, went on to the study of science, and obtained his doctorate in 1863. After serving as a volunteer in the 2nd Uhlan regiment of the royal guard, Paul Mendelssohn Bartholdy took up the study of chemistry together with Dr Martius in von Hofman's laboratory. He re-enlisted as a non-commissioned officer in the cavalry for the war with Austria in 1866. The battle of Königgrätz earned him his commission. With the advent of peace, he became deeply interested in modern processes of dye manufacture. As a result of his association with Dr Martius, he founded the important aniline factory at Rummelsburg. The Franco-Prussian war was once more the occasion for his re-enlistment. He was with the army of Prince Frederick-Charles at Orleans and he returned with the Iron Cross. Assiduous in his work, Paul Mendelssohn Bartholdy resumed his industrial activity and gave a new impetus to the Rummelsburg factory. He took over, on behalf of his business, the vast riverside works on the banks of the River Spree. It was on his initiative that the limited company for the manufacture of aniline was founded; in spite of the industrial crisis of 1880, this company was to become a concern of world importance. His enthusiasm for work and his courtesy in the most varied circles made him an outstanding personality, not only among his fellow-scientists in Germany, but also abroad, in France and elsewhere. A heart attack brought his life to an end in 1880, at the age of thirty-eight, the same age at which his father had died. His death was a grievous loss to Germany and brings to mind those words of Horace, in the Ode to Virgil, wherein the poet commemorates the death of Quinctilius Varus:

*'Quis desiderio sit Pudor, aut modus
Tam cari capitis.'*

Both his marriages were with members of the Oppenheim famliy. By his first marriage he had a son, Otto von Mendelssohn Bartholdy, born in Berlin in 1868. Otto von Mendelssohn Bartholdy became a well-known banker and was ennobled by William II; he was, however, unconnected with the banking house of *Mendelssohn & Co.* Having married his cousin, Cécile Mendelssohn Bartholdy, half-sister of Albrecht, mentioned earlier, he had a son and a daughter, Hugo and Cécile von Mendelssohn Bartholdy. By the second marriage of the great industrialist, Paul Mendelssohn Bartholdy, the composer's son, there were born Cécile, Lili, Louis, and Paul, who were in due course allied by marriage to the Gilbert, Passini, Speyer, and Nauheim families; in this branch of the family, there were no descendants to perpetuate the name of Mendelssohn Bartholdy.

The descendants of Paul, the composer's brother, were Gotthold (wife's maiden name Wentz) and Ernst von Mendelssohn-Bartholdy (wife's maiden name Warschauer), the latter having been ennobled. Finally, there was the latter's son, Paul von Mendelssohn-Bartholdy (wife's maiden name Lavergne), the last banker bearing the original name of Bartholdy to be actively interested in the old bank of *Mendelssohn & Co.*, of the Jägerstrasse in Berlin. But this famous bank still has a director of that name.[1]

---

[1] The famous bank of *Mendelssohn & Co.* was founded by Abraham Mendelssohn and Joseph Mendelssohn, the composer's uncle, in 1795; Joseph remained head of the bank until 1848. Then his descendants took over the management of this powerful enterprise; Alexander Mendelssohn, from 1821 to 1871; his son Franz von Mendelssohn (wife's maiden name Biarnez) from 1854 to 1889; Robert von Mendelssohn (wife's maiden name Giordigiani) from 1884 to 1917; Franz von Mendelssohn, Robert's brother (wife's maiden name Westphal) from 1892 to 1935; finally, Franz's son, Robert von Mendelssohn, is still to-day one of the partners of this banking house.

But the descendants of Joseph, Felix's uncle, shared the management of the bank's brilliant development with the Mendelssohn-Bartholdys (spelt with a hyphen; for the spelling of Mendelssohn Bartholdy, with or without a hyphen, see Chapter V, 'Art and Work'). Thus, after Abraham, Felix's father, who was a director of the bank from 1805 to 1821, the former's descendants succeeded him in the management of the banking house; Paul Mendelssohn-Bartholdy (wife's maiden name Heine) was a co-director from 1837 to 1874; his son, His Excellency Ernst von

The name of Cécile, so finely borne by Felix's wife, was chosen many times by succeeding generations in memory of their admirable forbear. On the genealogical trees of the Mendelssohn Bartholdy family, or, in the direct female line, of the Benecke and Wach families, veritable clusters of Céciles have grown, like bunches of perfumed flowers, and before them a regiment of Felixes have gracefully bowed ... On these branches, from which *music* and *happiness* have risen towards the sky, there have grown, too, in memory of Pastor Jeanrenaud's distinguished wife, many Elizabeths ...

And what has been the story of the Jeanrenauds, descendants of the famous pastor whose impressive personality has dominated these pages? The last male descendant of Charles, Cécile's brother, died at Miltenberg on the 17th of February, 1929, at the age of forty-six. He was a man of noble birth and a collector of military souvenirs. His sister, Mme Marie de Coulon-Jeanrenaud, who has descendants named Eschelbach, in America, and de Coulon, in Germany, now lives at Miltenberg in the Château de Grauberg. Other family relics and souvenirs passed into the hands of the de Bary [2] family by the marriage of Marie Jeanrenaud, Charles's daughter and Cécile's niece. The Souchay [3]

Mendelssohn-Bartholdy (wife's maiden name Warschauer), from 1871 to 1907. Finally, the last banker of this branch of the family, collateral with the composer's, was Paul von Mendelssohn-Bartholdy (first wife's maiden name Reichenheim, second wife's maiden name de Lavergne), who was at the head of *Mendelssohn & Co.* from 1902 to 1935. His widow still has an interest in this financial business, which carries with it the oldest and most solid German traditions.

[2] *The de Bary family.* Henri de Bary-Jeanrenaud, a Frankfurt banker, a generous resident of the town, and a firm supporter of the local French Church, came from a family of French refugees, originally from Tournay, whose name is to be found in documents as far back as the 12th century. In the course of time, the family received titles of nobility in Bavaria and Belgium. Frederick William II, king of Prussia, confirmed these ancient titles of nobility and incorporated them. Eight generations in succession lived in the aristocratic de Bary house in the Untermainkai. Henri de Bary had five children, including M. Henri de Bary, a Frankfurt banker, M. Carl de Bary, of Morges, Mme Koster de Bary, of Frankfurt, and Mme Deluz-de Bary, of Arcuse.

[3] *The Souchay family.* The famous senator, Edouard Souchay (wife's maiden name Schmidt), gave his name to a street in Frankfurt; he is the author of the journal from which I have quoted in the course of this narrative. He was an eloquent parliamentarian, a delegate from Frankfurt to monetary and customs conferences, and an administrator of the South German railways. One of his missions was to assist in the drawing up of the Schleswig and Holstein Statute. He has grandchildren still alive to-day in Marburg, one of whom is M. Theodore Souchay, who

and Hensel[1] families still have living descendants. But a study of the descendants of the Mendelssohn Bartholdy and Jeanrenaud families and of others united to them by marriage cannot rightly serve as a conclusion to this work.

The analysis of the great Mendelssohn Bartholdy's musical works has been made by acute critics. Nevertheless, there are one or two things which must be said about their analyses. Since the Englishman, Shedlock, set out his method of analysis and urged critics to distinguish in the first place the form or style of the spirit or sentiment which animates any musical work, it has been unanimously recognised that in Felix's compositions two

---

contributed greatly towards my documentation. This family of former refugees has representatives also in various towns in Germany and Great Britain. Senator Souchay and his sister Elisabeth Jeanrenaud-Souchay had not only Jean Souchay-Schunck, the brother, who has already been mentioned, but other brothers and sisters: Charles Souchay (wife's maiden name Detmar), Emilie Souchay (married name Fallenstein), Henriette Souchay (married name Benecke), and Auguste Souchay, who remained a bachelor. It can be seen that the family circle of Felix and Cécile Mendelssohn Bartholdy was a very extensive one.

[1] *The Hensel family.* The descendants of the Hensels through the marriage of Fanny Mendelssohn Bartholdy were also numerous and distinguished. In 1935, the academic world celebrated in Marburg the jubilee of Dr and Counsellor Kurth Hensel, member of the Leopoldine Academy (Halle) and various scientific societies. The Hensels were related to the Du Bois-Reymonds, German descendants of Felix-Henri Du Bois-Reymond, of Neuchâtel, who was born at Saint-Sulpice, in the Val-de-Travers, in 1782. Felix-Henri was one of the royalist malcontents in 1831 and became court counsellor to the king, in Berlin, and agent for the affairs of Neuchâtel; he died in 1865. His two sons, Emile and Paul Du Bois-Reymond, distinguished themselves, the one as professor of physiology and member of the Berlin Academy of Science, the other as professor of mathematics at Heidelberg. A number of the documents, manuscripts, paintings, and original drawings of Wilhelm Hensel, Felix Mendelssohn Bartholdy's brother-in-law, came, by marriage or inheritance, into the possession of the Reverend Pastor Paul Leo, of Osnabruck. His aunt, Mme Lili Du Bois-Reymond of Neubabelsberg, possesses an album of Fanny Hensel's in which her brother Felix wrote, at the age of twelve, a charming and still unpublished sonata. It is, in fact, the first he ever wrote. Two pages of the score are reproduced earlier in the book. It is an allegro piece in the genre of Mozart and Clementi, but romantic in conception; it was played in 1937 for the first time (along with the 'allegretto' composed during his honeymoon, at Freiburg im Breisgau in 1837) to illustrate my lectures at the University of Neuchâtel and my talks broadcast from Radio-Paris and Radio-Lausanne. The 'allegretto' of 1837 (in the honeymoon journal of the newly-married couple, now the property of the Wach family) could be entitled: '*Echange de frais bouquets de violettes*'. The sketch, or sonatina, of 1821, composed sixteen years earlier and dedicated by a schoolboy to his sister Fanny, though perhaps more remarkable for its handwriting than its substance, already shows a well-developed piano technique and heralds the appearance of a symphonic master. There are also to be found among these same Hensel manuscripts, now in the possession of the Du Bois-Reymond family, picturesque notes in the handwriting of Zelter, Paganini, Schlegel, Moscheles, and Jean Paul.

qualities have been supreme; variety and purity. By purity in music, do we not mean that quality which, by its perfection, dispenses with all associations that are foreign and inferior to the music? Wagner's music is at its best in the theatre. Mendelssohn's dispenses with theatrical effects; it is almost injured by them. What is necessary to enhance the music of *A Midsummer Night's Dream* is less the spectacle of Shakespeare's comedy than the memory of it. The music is so perfect a transformation of words into sound that the stage setting is irrelevant. Men of taste will, however, class Mendelssohn among musicians of the theatre—although he wrote little music specifically for this purpose—because his was a theatre of ideas, intelligence, humour, and art, shorn of all that is artificial, ridiculous, and grandiloquent on the stage. Mendelssohn himself gave no title to the 'Songs Without Words', which received their name from others after him; but the apposite title finally chosen indicates that these pieces can dispense with words and gestures. They are small, complete entities, melodic masterpieces of pure song; they are sufficient unto themselves and contrast with the works of so many other musicians, where the title of the music is often worth more than its substance.

Mendelssohn Bartholdy is classical in his style, and even more so in his modulation. At the same time, his thought is frequently romantic, with a romanticism that is not in the least morbid, but colourful and sparkling. The combination gives to his masterpieces a strange originality; Felix is both classical and romantic. He is a symbol *par excellence* of the transition between two epochs; in his work appear simultaneously the most finished qualities of both. Whereas in the work of Schubert and Schumann there is repetition, in Mendelssohn's there is development. If the symphony was perhaps handled with more power by Beethoven and Wagner, Felix had a passionate love of orchestration. The orchestra was linked with his musical thought, with his supreme idea, and with a will that was always sure of itself. He never permitted the divergences and the anarchy which have led so many other masters on to dangerous rocks, there to be overcome by a jumble of makeshift devices which were designed to replace true musical power.

Because Mendelssohn's music is at the same time traditional and modern, it will live and victoriously survive all controversy. The stupidities of fashion are well-known. How many snobs, without in the least understanding it, lavish praise on the magnificent music of Bach! These same people will say: 'Mendelssohn is not serious enough, not profound enough for us'. The reason is that they are incapable of grasping the solemn religious feeling, the sublime and immovable faith, the '*ethos*' of Mendelssohn's genius, which shows itself in so many movements animated with elegiac grace, expressing itself most often in minor key, deeply moving in its laments, its plaints, its harsh torment, its passion, and its

Bust of the composer.

disturbing melancholy. I speak now not only of the religious 'andante' of his *Italian Symphony*, or the *Reformation Symphony*, or the *Scottish Symphony*. Mendelssohn's unshakable faith and feeling, which sought the piano and the bible as their twin supports, were such that even in composing a work to celebrate the jubilee of a printing press—certainly a secular invention!—he made of it a sacred cantata.

Wagner, in spite of his unjust pamphlet, pays homage to Mendelssohn; he considers *Fingal's Cave* a remarkable descriptive masterpiece. But surely, on several occasions, his own music was inspired by Mendelssohn's? It is enough to think of the *Rheingold*, whose principal motif is the same, almost without alteration, as that of the overture to *Melusine*. And where did the ungrateful Wagner draw his inspiration for the fundamental melody of the dialogue between Brunnhilde and Siegmund in the second act of the *Valkyrie*, if not from the opening bars of the *Scottish Symphony*? Is there not a striking similarity between passages in *Tristan* and a certain episode in the *Lobgesang*? Here are certainly examples of Wagner giving substance to his own work by borrowing from Mendelssohn.

There is no question of placing Mendelssohn at the head of all; other masters have been as sublime and as profound—often more so. They have, too, been less popular and less widely understood. Yet did not *Saint Paul* and *Elijah* restore its great prestige to the oratorio? And how numerous have been the composers to follow the path laid down by Mendelssohn Bartholdy. The influence which he exercises over all German, Swiss, English, and American choral societies is still considerable. Whether they wish it or not, whether they sing his works or not, he is their spiritual father. To a melodic talent unequalled in Germany since Mozart and Schubert, Felix added a universal culture.

Various 'Mendelssohn Foundations' for the provision of scholarships to promising students have been created in Europe. In the minds and hearts of millions of men, have risen monuments to the memory of this artist who was so generous and likable, of this glorious poet permeated with the spirit of Shakespeare and Goethe.

The religious side of Mendelssohn's nature was strongly influenced by his study of Bach. Felix rescued Bach's music from public neglect. It was perhaps his example which led Schumann, Brahms, and even Wagner to a close study and admiration of Bach. Mendelssohn's initiative in revealing the greatness of Bach to Germany was indeed the starting-point of the entire present renaissance in the appreciation of Bach's work.

Monument of Mendelssohn Bartholdy
By Werner Stein, in front of the Leipzig Gewandhaus, destroyed by the Nazis.

Mendelssohn's dominating influence on Schumann is well known; it was from him that Schumann derived his lyricism and

Tomb of Cécile Mendelssohn Bartholdy
in the Frankfurt cemetery

romanticism. It is likewise undeniable that Brahms, while drawing much of his inspiration from Bach and Beethoven, felt the charm of Mendelssohn's music. Other composers of symphonies, Anton Rubinstein, Volkmann, Hermann Goetz, Rheinecke, and Dietrich, were also to some extent the musical descendants of Mendelssohn Bartholdy.

Although there are occasions when an artist cannot throw off certain sub-conscious racial influences, it has been claimed that Mendelssohn was, with Händel, the greatest of protestant musicians. However, the hitherto unknown personality of the wife of this famous creative artist could not but have been an important influence on his work. My aim was therefore to complete, as far as lay within my power, the excellent existing bibliography.

In making known this story of the inspiring marriage between these two distinguished beings, Felix Mendelssohn Bartholdy and Cécile Jeanrenaud, I have found it necessary to bring forward numerous documents which cast on the composer an unexpected light, at once more firm and more human. As far as possible, I have allowed the manuscripts to speak for themselves.

Mendelssohn Bartholdy, the son of a protestant, a protestant himself, an ardent German patriot, married a wife of his own faith, chosen from among the aristocracy of Frankfurt, and in doing so gave to the world a fine historical example of conjugal love, of love within the framework of morality and law; that framework from which so many artists have broken loose, with their wayward, discordant, and insecure liaisons, before which the neurotics of our generation bow down. The standards which this worthy and loyal genius set himself in marriage were as high in his sense of duty as in the magnificent edifice of his artistic effort. Mendelssohn does honour to his remotest origins, he does honour to the family, he does honour to Germany, to protestantism, to music. At the end of the score of *A Midsummer Night's Dream*, the famous *Wedding March*—the benediction given to three happy couples—was inspired by the inexpressible emotions of his own marriage; it was a reflection of his love, of the exquisite fusion of spirit which had taken place between Cécile and himself. It was left to future generations, to the hearts of innumerable beings who were later to be united amid the sound of that same music, as the sign and symbol of wisdom, of passion, and of perfect love.

The luminous wake of Mendelssohn's astonishing career gleamed in the dark fog of Europe after the Napoleonic wars; his immortal barque, white sails swollen with a virile romanticism, carried him and his triumphant work beyond all the oceans. A grateful world cannot be unmindful of the part played in this journey by his young wife, she who accompanied him among the crested waves; the pure, understanding, and beautiful Cécile Jeanrenaud, a being of poetry, tenderness, and greatness, eternally garlanded with roses.

SOURCES

A. MANUSCRIPTS; ORIGINAL DOCUMENTS

State and *Vénérable Classe* records, Neuchâtel.

Civic and official records, Frankfurt.

Civic records, Bâle.

Civic and Reformed Church records, Lyons.

Documents of Otto von Mendelssohn Bartholdy, Potsdam.

Documents of Mme Paul von Mendelssohn-Bartholdy, Berlin.

Documents of Dr Paul Benecke, Eastbourne and Oxford.

Papers of Mme Frédéric de Steiger, *née* Wach, Bâle.

Records and documents of the Wach family, Wilderswil, Radebeul and Murnau.

Letters and documents of Mme M. de Coulon-Jeanrenaud, Château de Grauberg, Miltenberg.

Documents of Félix Eschelbach, Rio de Janeiro.

Documents of Mrs. Albrecht Mendelssohn Bartholdy, Clifton Hampden, Oxford.

Documents of the Mendelssohn & Co. Bank, Berlin.

Papers and documents of Théodore Souchay, Marbourg.

Documents of John Edward Darnton, London.

Documents of Henry de Bary, Frankfurt.

Papers of Carl de Bary, Morges.

Documents of Mme Louise Deluz-de Bary, Areuse.

Documents of Robert Bory, Coppet.

Records and documents of Henry de Sandol-Roy, Couvet and Paris.

Documents of the Hensel, Léo and Du Bois-Reymond families, Osnabrück and Neubabelsberg.

Documents of the Appia family, Paris.

Documents of Georges-A. Bridel, Lausanne.

Papers of Dr Pierre Favarger, Mlle Elisabeth Jeanrenaud and Dr Charles Perrochet, Neuchâtel and La Chaux-de-Fonds.

Archives of Jacques Petitpierre, documents and papers: Vincent, Sandol, Würflein, Droz, de Meuron, d'Ivernois, Petitpierre, Jeanrenaud, Mendelssohn Bartholdy, Souchay, Wach, Le Chevalier de Rochefort and Touchon (Neuchâtel).

B. BIBLIOGRAPHY

Beiträge zur Genealogie Altfrankfurter Familien, Herbert de Bary (Baer & Co., Frankfurt a. M., 1922).

Die Familie Mendelssohn, 1729—1847, Sébastien Hensel (New edition, 2 vols. Im Insel-Verlag, Leipzig, 1924).

Fanny Mendelssohn, E. Sergy (Fischbacher, Paris, 1888).

Les Maîtres de la musique. Mendelssohn, Camille Bellaigue (Paris, 1907).

Mendelssohn, Camille Bellaigue (Alcan, Paris, 1920).

Felix Mendelssohn Bartholdy, Ernst Wolf ('Harmonie', Berlin, 1906).

Felix Mendelssohn Bartholdy, Briefe und *Reisebriefe*, Paul Mendelssohn Bartholdy (Leipzig, 1875, 1882).

Mendelssohn, Paul de Stœcklin (Laurens, Paris, 1927).

Une heure de musique avec Mendelssohn, Emile Vuillermoz (Aux Editions Cosmopolites, Paris).

Felix Mendelssohn Bartholdy, sa vie et ses œuvres, H. Barbedette (Au Ménestrel, Paris, 1868).

Felix Mendelssohn Bartholdy, Ferdinand Hiller (Du Mont-Schauberg, Cologne, 1874).

Felix Mendelssohn Bartholdy, Dr W. A. Lampadius (Leuckart, Leipzig, 1886).

Briefe an Ignaz und Charlotte Moscheles, Felix Mendelssohn Bartholdy, Leipzig, 1888).

Goethe-Jahrbuch XII, 1891 (9 letters of Mendelssohn).

Goethe und Mendelssohn, Dr Karl Mendelssohn Bartholdy (Hirzel, Leipzig).

Briefwechsel zwischen Goethe und Zelter, 6 vols. (Berlin, 1833—1834).

Lettres inédites de Mendelssohn, translated by A.-A. Rolland (Hetzel, Paris).

Felix Mendelssohn Bartholdy, sein Leben und seine Werke, Auguste Reissmann (Guttentag, Berlin).

Dictionary of Music, Hugo Reimann; art. *Mendelssohn.*

Joseph Joachim, A. Moser (Berlin, 1858).

On Music and Musicians, Robert Schumann (Dennis Dobson, 1947).

Meine Erinnerungen an Felix Mendelssohn Bartholdy, Eduard Devrient (Leipzig, 1869).

Dictionary of Music and Musicians, art. *Mendelssohn*, George Grove (London, 1879—1889).

Clara Schumann. Ein Künstlerleben, Litzmann. 2 vols. (Leipzig).

Voyageurs romantiques en pays neuchâtelois, Charles Guyot (Delachaux & Niestlé S. A., Neuchâtel and Paris).

Patrie Neuchâteloise, Vols. 1 and 2, Jacques Petitpierre (Imprimerie Centrale et Baconnière, Neuchâtel, 1934, 1935).

A Sketch of the Life and Works of the late Felix Mendelssohn Bartholdy, Julius Benedict, 2nd edition (London, 1853).

La musique en Allemagne. Mendelssohn, Camille Selden (Paris, 1867).

Die französische reformierte Gemeinde in Frankfurt am Main 1554—1904, dedicated to Henri de Bary-Jeanrenaud, by Frédéric-Clément Ebrard, Director of the Library (Ecklin, Frankfurt, 1906).

F. Mendelssohn Bartholdy, C. M. von Weber, Klassiker der Tonkunst, Dr Léopold Schmidt and Hedwig Neumayer (Universal-Edition, A.-G., Vienna).

Jenny Lind, C. A. Wilkens.

The von Schunck Family, John Edward Darnton (Privately printed and published, 1933).

Frankfurter Handelsgeschichte, Vols. II, IV and V, Dr Alexandre Dietz (1921, 1925).

La Reine Victoria, Abel Chevalley (Delagrave, Paris, 1902).

Georges Appia, 2 vols., preface by Wilfred Monod (Flammarion, Paris, 1910).

Mendelssohn and his Friends in Kensington, Mrs. Rosamund Brunel Gotch (Oxford University Press, London, 1934).

Histoire de la Musique, Charles Nef (Payot, Paris, 1931).

Moses Mendelssohn, Otto Zarec (Querido Verlag N. V., Amsterdam, 1936).